BUSINESS
FRAUD
KNOW IT & PREVENT IT

BUSINESS
FRAUD
KNOW IT & PREVENT IT

JAMES A. BLANCO
CERTIFIED QUESTIONED DOCUMENTS EXAMINER

Foreword by Detective Dave Evans (Ret.)
Sacramento County (California) Sheriff's Department

HUMANOMICS
PUBLISHING

Systems where People Matter

Library of Congress Number: 00-109015
ISBN (Hardbound): 0-9666085-3-4
ISBN (Softbound): 0-9666085-4-2

Editorial Coordination: Jennifer Adkins
Grace Associates, Ltd., at Publishers Place, Inc.
P.O. Box 2395
Huntington, West Virginia 25724

Cover and Book Design: Mark S. Phillips
Marketing+Design Group
www.marketingdesigngroup.com

First Edition

Printed in Canada

H⦶MANOMICS PUBLISHING

945 Fourth Avenue, Suite 200A
Huntington, WV 25701

FRAUD STATISTICS

Employee fraud against businesses accounts for $400 billion in annual losses.

Approximately 25% of the FBI's efforts are devoted to the investigation of white-collar crimes.

85% of all Internet purchases are made using credit cards, with an estimated ten trillion in total dollar transactions by the end of the year 2000. Yearly fraud losses average $580 per Internet shopper.

More than 1.4 million checks are forged every day, causing $27.3 million in daily losses to American businesses.

According to the National Check Fraud Center, check fraud and counterfeiting are among the fastest-growing problems affecting the nation's financial system, producing estimated annual losses of $10 billion and continuing to rise at an alarming rate.

A nationwide study of fraud found that 58% of survey respondents reported having experienced a fraud or an attempted fraud.

Respondents to a National Institute of Justice survey indicated that of those who fell prey to a fraud scheme, 85 percent lost money or property; 20 percent suffered financial or personal credit problems, and 14 percent suffered health or emotional problems.

500,000 people are victimized by identity theft every year, with the average time to clear their damaged credit records being two years. When victims were asked, "Did the police help you in any way?" 76% of respondents answered, "No."

Projected losses due to telemarketing and direct marketing fraud schemes alone are thought to be more than $40 billion annually.

The average bank robbery in this country nets $250, but the average high-tech crime nets at least $50,000.

Fraud in the insurance industry costs consumers $120 billion per year.

Motto to Remember: "Retention is better than apprehension."

SCAM ARTISTS DON'T WANT YOU TO READ THIS BOOK!

Dear Potential Victim:

This is a book I have wanted to write for you for years, but I have resisted the urge. After all, to reveal the methods of fraud and tell the related stories is to educate the rip-off artists by giving them new and better ways to commit their frauds. However, to not reveal the story is to leave you in the dark as to what is really happening out there, rendering you vulnerable to scam artists. Many times the minds and methods of criminals are so far ahead of honest citizens that we fall prey to their devices.

I hope you will take this message to heart and implement the practices outlined in this book. It is time to strike back against fraud by educating yourselves and bolstering up your defenses, because the attack is coming not only from outside your businesses, but also from within in the form of embezzlements by employees you think you can trust.

By discussing fraudulent documents as well as computer and Internet frauds, this book will show you how to safeguard yourself and your business against many of the forms of fraud. The con artists are lurking at your back windows, waiting for an opportunity to pounce. It is time to stop being "innocent as doves;" the time has come to be "shrewd as wolves."

Working to guard your resources,

James A. Blanco
Blanco Questioned Documents
Sacramento, California

Diplomate: American Board of
            Forensic Document Examiners

www.PreventFraud.net

FOREWORD

Jim Blanco knows whereof he speaks. I've followed Jim's career through his early days as a documents examiner with the Sacramento County Sheriff's office, an analyst with the Federal Bureau of Alcohol, Tobacco, and Firearms through his current work as an independent Questioned Documents Examiner. Jim now flies his own airplane to cases across the country, and sometimes even to Mexico and Canada.

I'm delighted to recommend his packaging of seventeen years plus of frontline experience into a book entitled *Business Fraud: Know It & Prevent It.*

This book should be required reading for anyone who owns or manages a business—*any* business.

As a fraud investigator myself for the past twenty-three years, both in law enforcement and in the private sector, I have seen too much suffering from people who thought they could trust everybody who did business with them. I've watched small businesses go under simply from the results of a scam. If a business, say a store, is operating on a fairly thin profit margin, and happens to be stretched tight already with its creditors, even taking in one bad $3,000 check can spell disaster.

Just think: you as a business owner spend hours and hours of your own time and staff time trying to get the best merchandise into your store or develop the best equipment processes for your plant or the best methods for your service company. However, you spend next to no time at all preparing your people to recognize fraud. It's true that 99 customers out of 100—or even more than that—will be perfectly honest. So it becomes easy to let your guard down.

That's what the fraudsters are counting on. Once your business requires the personal services of Jim Blanco or another investigator, you may already be in deep trouble.

Many business people suffer fraud losses quite needlessly. Now, simply by taking the time to read this book, or using it to train your people, you can save yourself many dollars and much heartache.

Business Fraud: Know It & Prevent It will greatly improve your chances of arming yourself and your people to spot the scams and stop them before they can hurt you.

Detective Dave Evans (Ret.)
Fraudulent Documents Bureau
Sacramento County Sheriff's Department
Sacramento, California

TABLE OF CONTENTS

TABLE OF CHECKLISTS

INTRODUCTION
Protect Yourself for Success

N one of us wants to lead "ordinary" lives; we want to lead "extraordinary" lives. We like the challenges of the fast-paced market place: second-guessing supply and demand problems, perhaps, or finding customer needs and filling them as only our businesses can. Detecting and filling specific needs, and doing so well, is how we become extraordinary. Meeting these challenges makes us better people, makes our businesses more productive and lucrative, and in the end, makes the world a better place.

What a great country we have in our United States of America! You can go into any kind of business you want—computer stores, imports, hobby shops, restaurants, rental yards, consulting firms, high finance—the business possibilities are limited only by your imagination. Dreams are just one step away from reality. If you want something enough, you can get it. If you can imagine it, it can come true.

BUT—you will achieve your goals and dreams only through patience, smart planning, realism, perseverance, and hardship. Yes, tragedy, despair, and heartache are dream ingredients. In fact, I would even say *terror* is an ingredient. In my earlier days I spent many sleepless nights wondering how I was going to make it through the next month financially. I've had anxiety attacks and even gone to the hospital, thinking I was really having a heart attack. I know about terror. But these difficult experiences we endure make us strong and toughen us up. Terror and looming tragedy can motivate us to greatness.

Recently I was flying my plane home from a business trip in Tijuana. It was night, and the weather was poor. I heard a pilot of a light aircraft in my same sector experiencing a moment of terror as he told Oakland Center, "My windshield is frosted over, and I think there's ice on the wings." Although I felt bad for him, I knew he could have prevented his moment of terror had he been better informed as to the flight conditions along his route. Having received a pilot's briefing before I departed, I knew enough to stay out of that altitude.

Knowledge and experience make the difference. Use information to identify the potholes, and use experience to successfully navigate around them. I don't consider myself an exceptionally smart person, just a persistent one. By spending time studying a scam, I can understand it as I take it apart piece by piece. Some frauds and scams are intricate and complex, but if you study them carefully, you'll master the building blocks that lead to understanding.

By drawing upon cases of others who have suffered, I have designed this book to steer you around the snares and dangers to get you to your destination in one piece. And if you have become tangled in a snare along the way, we'll talk about that too. I will have suggestions as to what to do and who to see when you have been the victim of fraud.

All the scams discussed in this book can hurt companies that have not put safeguards in place. A nationwide study of fraud found that 58% of survey respondents reported having experienced a fraud or an attempted fraud. In fact, every single scam discussed here has been worked against companies like yours. By studying them you can learn from the vulnerability and losses of others. I have been careful not to mention the actual names of victimized companies that were not matters of public record. At the same time, when relevant, I have tried to describe the kind of business so you can get a better understanding of the situation in which the scam was conducted.

Some scams, whether simple or complex, could mean an instant death blow to your company. Others could leech profits from your business over time. It all depends on your vulnerability and the scam committed against you while you were vulnerable. This book discusses scams that can be worked against a great variety of companies, large and small. There is something for everybody here. All levels of business owners and managers will benefit from reviewing these chapters.

"Fraudproof" your business

In our pursuit of excellence in our field and profitability in our business while our companies grow, we can become distracted with the day-to-day details of running the company. There are so many things to do that they absorb all our attention and energy. From time to time we have perhaps heard stories or read in the paper about others being the victims of fraud. Then we think, "This would never happen to *us*." The problem is that until we have been stung by a con artist, we give little or no thought to the possibility that we would ever be ripped off. We are probably the most vulnerable when the business is turning a good profit. That is when we are quite preoccupied and giving no thought to potential fraud. But this is exactly the time that we need to be sure our business is "fraudproof." Count on this book to show you how.

It could happen to you

When I tell people what I do for a living ("I'm a forgery examiner"), I am amazed at the replies I get. Most people respond, "You mean that really happens? People forge other people's names?" You bet they do. Forgery, counterfeiting, and fraudulent documents, as well as Internet fraud, are all part of the everyday workplace. Respondents to a National Institute of Justice survey indicated that of those who fell prey to a fraud scheme, 85 percent lost money or property; 20 percent suffered financial or personal credit problems, and 14 percent suffered health or emotional problems.

Just because it may not have happened to you—yet—don't dupe yourself into believing that it doesn't happen. It's like being struck by lightning: you may think it will never happen to you, but when it does happen it can be quick, painful and, after the smoke clears, sometimes lethal to your business.

Please trust me: I am not overstating the threat from fraudulent schemes. In a single report I filed with the Sacramento County Sheriff's Department, I listed several victims of the same scam artist. These merchant victims included two computer stores, a jewelry store, a tire store and motorcycle dealership, two electronics stores, two furniture stores, and a hobby store. All these businesses accepted counterfeited cashier's checks, and they suffered a combined loss of over $200,000!

As a Questioned Document Examiner, I have worked thousands of cases, both criminal and civil. In almost every case, some sort of deception was alleged. Did Grandpa really sign the will? Was the contract valid? Questions arise about signatures and handwriting on movie contracts, titles to antique race cars—altered and distorted contracts of all types.

Yet of all the interesting cases I've worked, perhaps the most devastating ones concerned the destruction of small businesses by crooks who defrauded the business owner. The Federal Trade Commission has estimated that Americans and Canadians lose over *forty billion dollars* each year to scam artists! A great percentage of these losses could have been prevented if the steps outlined in this book had been followed.

Even today, as I was writing this introduction, a manager brought a case into my office involving employee deception. Interestingly, the supervisor informed me that the company owner was not too concerned about the situation because, although it was a matter of deception and fraud against the company, the loss was nominal. Beware: when employees get the message that any kind of fraud is tolerated by managers or the company owner, they will move up to bigger scams.

When examining embezzlement cases, I have seen the same pattern time and again: employees try to pass off a couple of fraudulent vouchers, invoices or checks, just to see if they can get away with it. When they discover that they *can* get away with such things, those same employees then repeat the fraud in much higher dollar amounts. A lax attitude about such scams creates a fertile ground for business losses.

Some company owners are totally immersed in the excitement and activity of their newfound success; others reaped success years ago and are now distracted by other businesses or leisure time pursuits and would really rather not be bothered with the day-to-day running of their companies. In either event, business owners, as well as supervisors and accountants, should not neglect the internal security of their companies. Left unchecked, small losses can become overwhelming losses as employees get the message that it is OK to defraud the company from within, even as other rip-off artists take advantage of your company's vulnerabilities from the outside. You need the tools to put preventative safeguards in place and maintain them.

In these chapters I will not only describe different types of scams, but I will also cover things to look out for to prevent your business from being victimized. I will tell you where to look for weaknesses in your company, and I will outline everyday protections that you can put in place as an immediate, proactive step to begin protecting your assets right away. If you are an attorney who deals in contract fraud and business litigation, this book will provide you with the tools to better represent your clients.

Just remember this: "Where there is light, there are bugs." If you are running a successful business, you will be attracting the unscrupulous. So let's get armed for the mission of "fraud-proofing." We will start by getting inside the criminal mind to see how he (or she) thinks and operates.

ACKNOWLEDGMENTS

*"It requires a great deal of boldness and a great deal of caution
to make a great fortune, and when you have it,
it requires ten times as much skill to keep it.*

— Ralph Waldo Emerson

Although it is difficult to say what makes a person who and what he is today, I believe that it can be wrapped up in the word, "People." When I think back to those who have contributed to and influenced my career in the field of Questioned Documents, I must first mention Terrence Pascoe, my trainer and mentor; Mary Riker, my colleague at the Federal Bureau of Alcohol, Tobacco and Firearms at the Western Regional Forensic Science Crime Laboratory; and my fellow workers, Bill Connor, David Crowe, and Marty Collins at the California Dept. of Justice Bureau of Forensic Services.

There are countless Special Agents, Detectives, Investigators and Attorneys who through the great teacher of casework itself have helped me to gain a practical understanding of the applications of forensic documents to the realities of life and law, whether municipal, state, federal, military or international law. These people include:

Bill Cramer, retired Detective with the Sacramento Sheriff's Dept.; former Assemblyman Larry Bowler, who was the Commander of the old Fraudulent Documents Bureau where I started out; the ATF Special Agents at the Tulsa Post of Duty, "smartest POD in the field;" Attorney John DuToit, brilliant legal mind, Johannesburg, S. Africa; Eduardo Roy, former U.S. Attorney in San Francisco, now in private practice.

I here express my appreciation also to those who contributed through discussions of the subject matter, and to those who reviewed and commented on the manuscript versions of this book. These people are: Jimmy Smith Sr., Forensic Document Examiner, Las Vegas Metropolitan Police Department; Pat McCarthy, Senior Investigator, U.S. Bank Corporate Security, Minneapolis, Minn.; Leon Malinofsky, Computer Guru, TechnologyForensics.com, Northampton, Mass.; Dale M. Lee, Chief Investigator California State Controller's Office; Supervising Sergeant Vern Wallace and Detective Al Henschel with the Sacramento Sheriff's Financial Crimes Bureau; Resty Manapat of Costco Wholesale; my trainee, Tiffany Laverty, who, upon completion of her Master of Forensic Science degree, has left my practice for the Federal Triangle in Washington, D.C., as an upcoming Questioned Documents Examiner; and finally, my son Austin Blanco, computer wizard and creative thinker in his own right.

A special word of thanks is due to my dedicated and hard-working editor, Jennifer Adkins. Through countless phone calls and e-mail volleys I have come to appreciate her as a brilliant organizer with a rich understanding and mastery of the English language.

To all the named and the many unnamed, "Thanks beyond what words can convey."

DISCLAIMER

The information in this book is not offered as legal advice, but is offered from the perspective of a professional Questioned Document Expert who has observed the personal and business losses of people around the country and world. The implementing of the advice in this book will instill precautions into business and personal commerce and will help to reduce fraud attacks against the reader. However, it is suggested that the reader consult an appropriate attorney when confronted with any issues that may lead to legal proceedings.

This book is not to be construed as a primer or treatise to prepare anyone to be a Forensic Questioned Document Examiner. Such expertise cannot be learned by reading a single book or through correspondence courses, but must be learned under the watchful tutelage of a Journey Level Examiner for a period of no less than two years of full-time training solely in the field of questioned document examinations.

ONE

GENERAL FRAUD TECHNIQUES

Understanding the Methods of the Con Artists

Before getting into the nitty-gritty of actual scams, it is important to understand some basics of how swindlers work their craft. There are many creative ways to apply these fundamental scam techniques, but once you have an understanding of the basics, the frauds I discuss later will make more sense.

Most types of fraud involve the distortion of some sort of document. A document, however, is not just an 8 $^{1}/_{2}$" x 11" sheet of paper: it may also be a receipt, a voucher, an invoice, a note, or even a torn scrap of paper. Also, keep in mind that scams don't only revolve around forged signatures. Other aspects of documents can be manipulated as well, such as the typewriting or the computer-printed text. Forms can be replicated, rubber stamp impressions can be faked (including notary stamps)—in fact, anything your eye can see on a document can be distorted toward fraudulent ends. We will begin here by talking about the fraudulent use of signatures.

FORGERY

Who would have thought that meandering lines on papers would have become so important to our day-to-day living? No wonder there is so much forgery in our world, as it is the forger who has the better understanding of the value of signatures and documents than we honest citizens.

He is the one who by deception and fraud uses his forgery techniques to alter reality in his favor. Through forgery, he takes what he wants. The land, home, boat, car, business, or bank accounts that were once part of your reality have now been transferred to the forger's world, where he quickly liquidates them and then vanishes before you know what hit you.

Figure 1.1

Figure 1.1 depicts the forged Howard Hughes signature on the famous "Mormon Will."

One such forger made an interesting attempt to steal a portion of the estate of Howard Hughes. Famous recluse Howard Hughes died in 1976, leaving no discoverable will. A bitter struggle ensued by thousands of people to claim his $6 billion fortune. Two powerful groups led the contenders. On one side was Will Lummis, a cousin of the billionaire, along with twenty other cousins claiming legal heirship, while on the other side were the people, led by Chester Davis, who had managed the empire of Howard Hughes for the last six years of his life.

While attorneys and executives of Hughes' corporations scrambled to find a will, speculation ran rampant throughout the country. One possibility was that Hughes had written a "holographic" will, which is a will written totally by hand (see Chapter 12). Shortly after this information was published, an alleged holographic will of Howard Hughes was found, left anonymously on a desk in the office building of the Mormon Church.

One provision of this will was that a 1/16th share of the estate would go to Melvin Dummar of Gabbs, Nevada. Melvin Dummar and his wife owned and operated a small gas station in Willard, Utah. He told reporters that years previously, he had picked up a bum in the desert who claimed to be Howard Hughes and that he had given this man a ride into Las Vegas and dropped him off behind the Sands Hotel after giving the man what spare change he had in his own pocket. Mr. Dummar claimed that later, a mysterious man drove into his service station and gave him the will, along with several pages of instructions. Mr. Dummar admitted that in following these instructions (which he had since burned), he had placed the will in an envelope and delivered it to the Mormon Church offices.

At least four prominent American Questioned Document Examiners concluded that the will was forged. In the end, the court ruled that the will was a forgery and that the billionaire, Howard Hughes, had died intestate (without leaving a will). Both Texas and California claimed Howard Hughes as a resident, which resulted in years of litigation that went several times to the U.S. Supreme Court. The issue was finally resolved with Texas receiving $50 million and California receiving $119 million. In 1983, after seven years of litigation, the heirs at law, led by Will Lummis, finally received the first of their inheritance from the estate.

Forgery, simply defined, is "to reproduce for deceptive purposes." Appendix D gives a more complete description as to what forgery is. When we think of forgery, we usually think of a scam artist writing someone else's name on a check or a contract. In our discussions of forgery in this book, I will usually be referring to the act of writing or copying someone else's signature without his or her permission or knowledge.

Forgers come in all flavors: the sloppy, the quick, the cunning, the patient, and the refined. The result is always the same, though—sleepless nights for the victim as he wonders how he is going to undo what has now been done. I even had a case where an attorney forged his client's name to a document, whereby he then took over his client's business and kicked her out of her own company! Of course, the jury took a dim view of his actions and, after I testified against him, awarded this woman large punitive damages. I was able to demonstrate to the court that the company owner's signature had been forged on the document, and further, that this particular attorney was the person who had forged it.

This story demonstrates the need to be vigilant against the dangers of forgery. Be on your guard, and put safeguards in place to protect yourself and your company. You can learn more about protecting your signature from forgery in Chapter 3.

COUNTERFEITING

Counterfeiting is defined as "an imitation designed to pass as an original," or the unauthorized duplication of a negotiable instrument with the intent to defraud. The term "counterfeit" can apply not only to U.S. currency, but to any document, certificate, coupon, or any kind of paper that can be illegitimately reproduced. A "negotiable instrument" is any paper item that can be exchanged for money, whether it be a personal check, cashier's check, money order, warrant, or any similar item that transfers monetary value.

Counterfeit negotiable instruments, then, are also such items as traveler's checks, money orders, business and personal checks, stock certificates, gift certificates, food stamps, welfare checks, and airline vouchers. Non-negotiable counterfeit documents can be birth certificates, college transcripts, diplomas, business licenses, immigration papers, or vehicle titles. Even your company forms, such as invoices, vouchers, quotes, and receipts, can be counterfeited

The counterfeiter has two hurdles to overcome. First, he must do a reasonable job imitating the paper stock of the true item to be counterfeited. Second, he must use a printing technology that will result in a finished product that imitates the ink, font, and any graphics on the document so as to fool the person who is being duped into accepting it as an authentic original.

Counterfeiting can be accomplished either by using the same paper source that is used for valid documents of the same kind, or by using imitations of that paper. For example, there have been instances of birth certificate stock paper disappearing from a county recorder's office, even though it is kept in a vault. This paper has a street value of $1,000 per sheet—and no wonder, since a person can establish an entire new identity with that single sheet of paper! All one has to do is to type up a birth record using any name of one's choosing, and with that record one can then obtain an identification or driver's license through the Department of Motor Vehicles. The counterfeiter can also obtain a valid social security number with this bogus birth certificate.

It is usually difficult to obtain the correct paper stock of the item to be counterfeited, however, so the next best option is to obtain paper that is similar to the authentic paper stock. With the vast number of paper stocks available today, a counterfeiter does not have to look very far to find an acceptable substitute paper. In many situations, such as the counterfeiting of negotiable instruments, the counterfeiter, like the forger, is not trying to fool the expert; he is just trying to fool the person at the point of negotiation to buy enough time for funds to transfer hands.

The second hurdle the counterfeiter must overcome is finding a printing technology that will result in a finished product that imitates the ink, font, and graphics on the document to be counterfeited. There are numerous printing technologies used today. One is the traditional print-shop method of offset lithography, in which a rubber-covered offset cylinder rolls over an inked plate, picking up the ink and then depositing it onto the paper. This method is used to create numerous forms, such as doctor's prescription pads, invoices, or job applications.

Then there are photocopy machine methods, which usually involve a dry toner process call "xerographic" printing. The word is derived from the Greek words "xeros," meaning "dry," and "graphos," meaning "writing." There are also different types of computer printer technologies, including daisy wheel, dot-matrix, ink-jet, and laser. Laser printing is really a xerographic process, so its printed results are very similar to those of photocopy machines.

Many counterfeiters master such processes to make checks and other bogus instruments appear authentic. However, just because a business check appears authentic, with typing on it and an "original" signature, or even if it has been stamped "The Sum of xxx" by a Paymaster checkwriter (also called a "check-protector"), that does not make the check authentic.

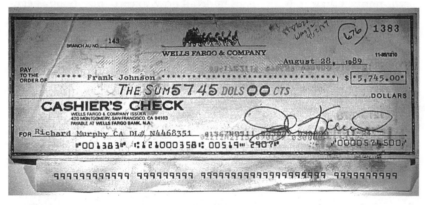

Figure 1.2

Figure 1.2 depicts a counterfeited check. This check appeared authentic enough because the paper was similar to normal paper stock used by the banks, and it had a combination of typing and a written amount imprinted by a check-writer machine. The problem with this check was that it exhibited a Wells Fargo logo of the stagecoach, but the bank routing number was for Bank of America. This was a composite counterfeited check.

One con artist routinely searched the classifieds for people who were selling diamonds. He would meet with the seller, check the ring, and then tell the seller that he had to go to the bank to get a cashier's check. Many people were surprised when they found out that the checks he later brought them were counterfeited. Their losses averaged $5,000 per instance.

As far as U.S. currency is concerned, watch out for denominations of $20, $50 and $100. These bills can simply be color copied and then negotiated. These denominations are easy to pass off because they attract little scrutiny from tellers and cashiers. Although many copy stores claim they exercise control over the use of their sophisticated color copying machines, it is still pretty easy to get one's hands on these machines and make all the copies one wants.

I have worked many cases where such items as American Express and Bank of America Visa traveler's checks have been color copied and then passed. If you accept these bogus instruments, you will remain the victim since these companies will not reimburse you for accepting counterfeited instruments. Chapter 6 discusses in detail how to recognize bogus negotiable instruments.

ALTERATIONS

When numbers or words are changed by taking something away or by adding something to the original, then the document has been altered. In such cases, the crook uses an authentic document after changing certain original entries in some way. For example, a business issued a small check in the amount of $300. It was subsequently altered on the numeric line by simply adding a "1" to make it $1,300. On the legal line (written amount line), there was enough space in the word "three" to put an "i" between the "h" and "r", a "t" between the "r" and "e," and add an "n" after the second "e," thus altering the original "three" to "thirteen."

In such ways business and personal checks, traveler's checks, and money orders can be "raised" by altering the amounts on the legitimate instruments. A trick that ex-cons learn in the "big house" is to purchase $1 money orders and then, by using a color of ink similar to that used by the check writer machine, they raise the amount to $100 or higher. The correct paper stock offers the look and feel of an authentic money order, but the numbers have simply been changed. Also, payees can be altered on stolen checks that have been put in the mailbox after people have written out their checks to pay bills.

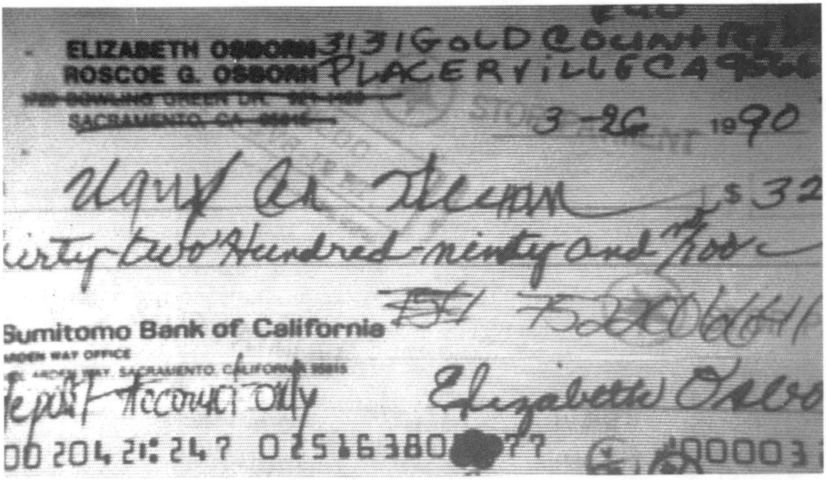

Figure 1.3
Image of the altered check as it appeared to the naked eye. The black ink used to alter the check was so similar to the original ink used that the human eye could not tell a difference.

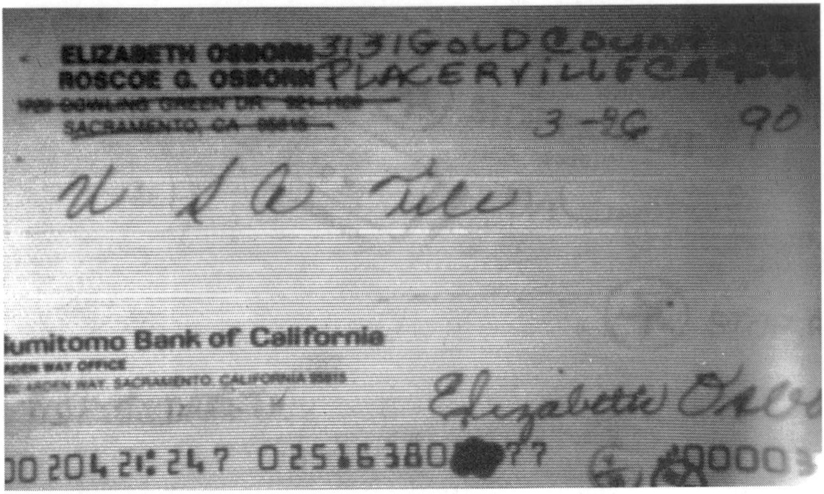

Figure 1.4
Image of check as it was originally filled out before being altered. Infrared imaging removes the added inks, thus restoring the image to its original unaltered condition.

Figure 1.4 (previous page) shows that a check was filled out making "USA Tile" the payee. However, a clever thief incorporated his own name around these letters, making the check payable to himself, "Nguyen Thuan." Figure 1.3 is a photograph under regular light showing what the unaided eye sees. However, Figure 1.4 is a photograph taken using an infrared barrier filter, which eliminated the added writing that changed the payee, restoring the check to its original appearance. A more detailed explanation of this infrared process can be found in Chapter 10.

In another example of using alteration to commit fraud, the owner of a Laundromat in southern California experienced a fire which destroyed his business. He submitted a business income interruption claim to his insurance carrier, with which he provided a record of his daily receipts covering the preceding three years. The insurance company, suspecting that these amounts had been raised by alteration, sent me the original documents for examination. Infrared and microscopic examinations revealed that the original entries had been raised substantially. In fact, when I had catalogued over $35,000 in raised amounts, I showed the insurance carrier my findings. Needless to say, this insurance company did not honor this fraudulent claim.

In an alteration fraud perpetrated by an employee, the suspect re-typed a paragraph of one of the pages of the company's employee policy manual, thus changing the definition of the work week. At a labor hearing, this altered policy manual was produced by the employee as the copy that the company had allegedly given to him when he was hired. The changes basically excused the bad conduct of the employee so as to eliminate cause for termination. The altered area looked fairly consistent with the rest of the page, except that the alignment of the "corrected" paragraph was not consistent with the original paragraphs.

Alteration is also used in embezzlement schemes. A school district used bank bag log sheets that showed money bag deposits. The person running the money to the bank altered one of the bag numbers on a log sheet, using white-out to cover the original entry, then drawing different numbers over the top. After altering the log, the suspect exchanged a larger bag of money with a smaller one. He skimmed off the difference when he took the money to the bank for deposit in the school district's treasury account.

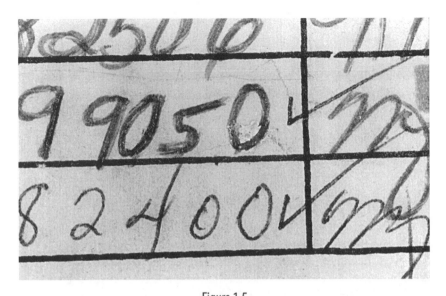

Figure 1.5

Figure 1.5 shows the altered entry of "99050." The original entry was "99156."

Figure 1.6

Figure 1.6 is a photomicrograph of the reverse side of the Figure 1.5 entry. At the bottom of the "0" one observes a tail that is the remnant of the original number "1."

Microscopic examination of the reverse side of this altered entry revealed an intersection of embossed lines. As when two lines are drawn in the sand with a stick, the second line drawn creates ridges up against the first line drawn. I was able to establish the first number written by examining the ridges against the number "1." Having deciphered the original numeric entry, I then passed this information on to the investigator, who was able to determine who had delivered the bag on that day.

SUBSTITUTIONS

A substitution occurs when a page is removed from a contract and a "revised" page is inserted in its place. The purpose is to change the meaning of the agreement in favor of the proponent (the person presenting this bogus document). For example, I once worked on a multi-page trust document in which various pages had been substituted. The authentic set of documents had been prepared using a laser printer. However, the bogus pages were printed by an ink-jet printer.

The attorney who brought me the case suspected that something was wrong with the trust, but he wasn't sure what it was because the creator of the bogus substituted pages had done a fairly good job of approximating the font design and text layout. When I showed him the differences in ink response under infrared examination, the attorney asked, "Can you print that out?" I told him, "Certainly."

Infrared examinations of printer inks may show that two pages are different. Under infrared examination, if one ink remains visible while the another ink disappears, then we know that their chemistry is different, and we know that they were not printed at the same time or by the same machine.

ADDITIONS

An "addition" occurs when characters, words or entire lines of text are added to a document. Additions may change subtle areas of an agreement, or they may change the numeric values or even the entire concept of a document. There are trade secrets I use to determine whether or not an addition has been made to a document.

Here is one humorous example of an addition: a young college student was about to go to the lake with his friends, but first he needed to cash his check at the bank. While he was talking with his friends, he endorsed his check and left it on the counter while he went into his room to get his keys. During the short time he was in the back room, one of his friends wrote under his endorsement name, "This is a bank robbery."

When the unsuspecting young man went into the bank and tried to cash his check, he ended up on the floor with a gun in his ear. This simple "addition" to this check, though in jest, shook up a lot of people that day. Fortunately, everybody went home in one piece and stayed out of jail. . . this time!

We must not forget that words convey thought and intent. Even short phrases or simple words can change the meaning of a document, whether written legitimately with everyone's knowledge and approval, or whether written for the purpose of fraud.

INTERLINEATIONS

Interlineations are additions inserted between lines of text. Interlineations are usually handwritten phrases or sentences squeezed in between the original entries on a document. These may, of course, have been added legitimately to a contract after the agreement has been initially prepared. In this case, it is customary that the parties initial the interlineations. Conversely, an interlineation may have been inserted by one of the parties at a later time to change things his or her way. If initials by the parties being defrauded accompany a bogus interlineation, those initials are usually forged.

If an interlineation becomes "questioned" or disputed between the parties, the task at hand is to identify the writer of the entry. Handwriting samples are obtained from the involved parties and any other persons suspected of writing this text. In this case, the party raising the objection to the interlineation can at least show that he was not the person who wrote it. This casts strong suspicion on the proponent of the interlineation—that is, the person most likely to benefit from it.

Further issues involve the presence or absence of approving initials by the parties. If the interlineation lacks the opponent's initials and the text was in fact written by the proponent or his agent/cohort, then the argument can certainly be made that the interlineation was not approved by the opponent but added at a later time.

If the disputed interlineation is accompanied by initials allegedly written by the parties, then the task is to determine whether or not the initials are all authentic. Of course, the initials of the proponents would be presumed authentic since they are the ones who prepared the interlineation, but the opponents' initials should be compared with known standards to see if they are authentic. If they were not written by the opponent, then one must determine whether any of the proponents forged the opponents' initials on the document.

In one example of a fraudulent interlineation, a towing company signed a lease to occupy a building that included parking accommodations for the workers and for customers. The facility was in a complex used by other tenants. The owner of the towing business built a fence around a portion of the parking area, according to the terms of a later modified lease which had been agreed to by the parties. However, the landlord later decided that he did not like the arrangement and inserted handwritten interlineations between the original typed text, then forged the initials of the tenant. The resulting changes modified the lease so that it put a great financial hardship on this business owner, and the matter went to court. A handwriting examination of the initials demonstrated in court that the landlord had indeed forged the initials of the tenant.

I hope these examples demonstrate that documents affect businesses, and people's lives, in critical ways. It is difficult enough to deal with customer needs, supply and demand problems, and employee disputes. We don't need the added stress of challenges, mediations, and litigation due to bogus documents. Now that you understand some basic fraud techniques, let's learn how documents are analyzed to determine their authenticity.

TWO

MATERIALS FOR MANIPULATION

Analyzing a Questioned Document

D ocuments, you might say, make the world go round, and there are many types. Financial documents include business and personal checks, payroll checks, money orders, cashier's checks, traveler's checks, credit card receipts, invoices, check cashing cards, ledgers, journals, check registers, vouchers, purchase orders, bank statements, and financial records. Real estate and probate documents may include deeds, promissory notes, reconveyances, leases, wills, codicils, trusts, and powers of attorney. Then there are identifications such as DMV driver's licenses and IDs, social security cards, and military IDs. All of these documents can be forged or criminally altered. I have listed in Appendix C the California Penal Codes section on forgery (470 (d)), which is quite similar to the codes in states around the country. It describes many, but by no means all, documents affected by forgery.

As you can see, there are more documents out there than you may have imagined. Just when I think I've seen it all, a new case comes in the door involving a document I never knew existed. For example, I recently worked one case involving a famous race horse that was stolen and removed from the country by means of a forged signature on a U.S. Trotting Association Certificate of Registration. Some time later I worked a different case in which a herd of cattle had been stolen by means of a forged Transfer of Brand document. An antique Mercedes race car, a movie contract, and a famous painting were also the subjects of "questioned document examinations." A document whose authenticity comes under some question is called a "questioned document" until such time as its authenticity is established.

There are many different ways of analyzing a document in order to determine whether it has been tampered with, is completely bogus, or is indeed legitimate. The following discussion of materials and methods will help you to understand how criminals operate and how professional investigators can detect their scams. This should enable you to better protect yourself and your business from fraud.

Some quick definitions to get us started (refer also to the glossary at the back of the book):

A *questioned document* is a document that has come under some sort of dispute. It may be just a signature or one thing on the document that is in question, or it may be the entire document.

A *known document* is the document that is a control sample. It may be an example of what an authentic form is supposed to look like, or it may be a document containing a true signature sample if signatures are the only thing in question.

An *exemplar* is a document containing handwriting or signatures given by a person for a particular reason. The person has been asked to give a writing sample to be compared with writing on the questioned document. This is also called a "request" sample since the writer was asked to give a sample and is now complying.

Keep in mind that anything observed during any of the following examinations can be recorded for future use, whether by means of regular emulsion film (such as 35 mm) while shooting pictures on a copy stand, or even through the eye of the microscope to show minute detail. Even digital infrared macro-photographs can be enlarged onto court exhibits to substantiate any observations made during such examinations.

Now let's examine some of the ways that documents can be analyzed.

Inventory of Submitted Evidence

The first thing I look for is a sign that any documents may be missing from the original file. I find answers to such questions as, Does the page numbering (if any) make sense? Do the dates from page to page portray a consistent and believable record? Are the original file documents in their order consistent with deposition testimony?

Examination of Printing/Machine Processes

In these examinations I attempt to answer the question, Have any original document pages been substituted by counterfeiting? (See Chapter 1.) I also see if there are composite documents and try to determine the possible sources from other documents already in the file. A composite document is a two-part document with at least one of the portions being a cut-and-paste recycling of a portion of another legitimate page.

I always examine the pre-printed forms to determine if someone has recreated a certain page to "clean up" a medical chart or some other type of document. In this examination I evaluate the printing processes used to create the forms. If the non-disputed pages were produced by means of offset lithography and have a form number, I evaluate all of the questioned pages to see if they share this same printing process and share the same form number on the same location as the other pages. Perhaps the questioned pages were created by using a photocopy or color copy machine in order to "clean up" the original record. This is where microscopes and experience team up to answer such questions.

Photocopy Process Examination

Photocopy machines leave extraneous toner markings that we document examiners affectionately call "trash marks." Perhaps you have seen these marks on documents before. They show up on paper as the result of photocopier defects, such as hot spots on the corona wire, drum defects, lint on the optics, or debris on the glass platen where one places the document to be copied.

I examine document pages to see if any such marks are present or absent. This examination can answer the question of the origin and consistency of the pages. For example, if the resource form pages themselves were legitimately created to begin with by being photocopied at one time and then used as stock material, a photocopy process examination can show whether or not all of the pages are consistent with one another.

This examination can isolate a common source machine and may also establish date parameters. Photocopy process examinations might also show that the questioned page was really a reconstructed page which does not match the other document pages. Conversely, it might show that there is nothing wrong with the questioned page and that the attack against it is without foundation.

Paper Examination

Beyond the question of printing processes used to print the words, borders, and logos on a form page is the question of paper. Is the kind of paper that was used for the remaining pages the same as that of the questioned sheet? Is there a watermark in the paper? What are its ultraviolet properties? Are there microscopic cutting bar marks along any edges that are either consistent or inconsistent? The answers to such questions can reveal whether the questioned sheet is actually a page that has been later inserted.

Paper is manufactured in different ways and, for example, can be regular bond paper or laid paper. These processes yield noticeably different papers. Bond paper is plain with no texture, whereas laid paper has faint vertical lines on one side and texture on the other side. If a bond paper was the legitimate paper source for all of the document pages, but the questioned sheet is laid paper or contains a watermark, then that fact alone could be quite revealing.

Examination of Mechanical Printing

If document pages exhibit mechanical typed text on them, then it is important to determine what type of printing device was used. The typing on the page may have been created by a mechanical typewriter or by a computer printer, whether dot-matrix, daisy wheel, ink jet, laser (xerographic), or a thermal process. Was the typing device that was used available to consumers before the date of the questioned typed entries, or was the device that typed the questioned text not available until several years after the alleged date? In other words, can it be shown that the typed text was backdated? In a classic case of backdating a document, in early 1999 the defendant was accused of forging documents that tied John F. Kennedy with Marilyn Monroe. The problem was that the typeface on these documents was from a typewriter not manufactured until the 1970s, which of course was many years later than when the documents were allegedly created.

A further question to resolve is whether or not a ribbon was also used in the ink transfer process, and if so, what type: was it an old cloth ribbon, or a single-strike correctable carbon film ribbon? Any discrepancies would be significant. By the way, ribbon cartridges from any suspect typewriters can be cracked open and the ribbon read to see if any of the typing on the questioned document matches any of the text on the ribbon. An analysis of the other entries on the ribbon which surround the questioned entry could then demonstrate if the questioned text has been backdated.

A computer itself can also be "cracked open," in a manner of speaking, by a computer technician in order to search for a text match. That is, the questioned text on the paper document might be matched to a computer file on the suspect's computer. If the file is found, its properties could be viewed, and this inspection could establish the file's date. The question at that juncture would be whether or not the computer file date is consistent with the date on the document.

Examination of Rubber Stamp Impressions

Rubber stamps can be counterfeited, and their impressions can also be feigned. Rubber stamps usually leave some peculiar indication as to their identity. Such indications can be significant in the attempt to determine if a stamp impression is truly authentic. Authentic rubber stamp impressions can also be cut off of legitimate documents and pasted on a bogus document to lend it an air of authenticity.

Rubber stamp impressions can provide significant chronological evidence as well. Rubber stamps show wear over time, and the wear patterns can be catalogued and potentially dated. If a rubber stamp purchased in 1989 was still being used in 1999, the impression made ten years later wouldn't look as crisp and clean as the renditions made when the stamp was first put in use. Therefore, if such a rubber stamp was used in 1999 to recreate an older record of say, 1992, it could be shown that the impression does not conform to the chronological evidence, so the document must have been backdated.

Infrared Examinations of Inks

The purpose of infrared examinations of inks is to evaluate whether or not two inks have similar properties or are definitely different. This examination is key when dealing with alterations, additions, or corrections to contracts or other documents. When examining a medical chart, for example, one would expect authentic, course-of-business charts to exhibit various inks even on the same page, and certainly throughout the entire chart. When a patient enters the internal waiting room, a nurse comes in and takes the blood pressure reading and temperature and writes these in the chart, along with entries of any symptoms. Afterwards the doctor enters the room and examines the patient, then writes notes and findings and recommendations in the record. It would be typical that the nurse and doctor would be using different pens of their own liking, and that they each might use different pens at different times.

In any event, similar records should exhibit differences in the usage of writing implements over time. Infrared examinations of authentic records would confirm the usage of different writing implements on these pages. On the other hand, would it not be strange to find that an entire medical chart over a ten-year period exhibited no differences in the pens being used? This would suggest that the entire file was destroyed and recreated in one sitting. Read more about medical fraud in Chapter 10.

Examination of Folds/Crease Marks, Punch Holes, Staples, and Tape

In a contract, agreement, will, trust, or other type of document, if a new sheet has been recreated as a "replacement" for an old sheet that has now disappeared, the new sheet will probably not match the folds and crease marks that appear on the original documents that have been residing in the file over time. Further, punch holes, if they exist, will probably not match the size and location of the other punch holes, and the questioned page may not have been punched by the same punch hole tool as the authentic pages in the document.

Additionally, the presence or lack of certain staples and/or staple holes can be extremely significant. Questioned document examiners can even be fooled by "secondary staple holes" found on documents. The examiner might improperly assume that certain pages bore additional staples at one time, rendering them different from the other pages in the file. This could prove to be a big bomb during litigation, so choose your expert wisely!

In Figure 2.1 at right, staple holes and imperfections in machine printing defects can not only identify a document, but also demonstrate association or lack of association with other documents, as well as establishing dating parameters within which the document was created.

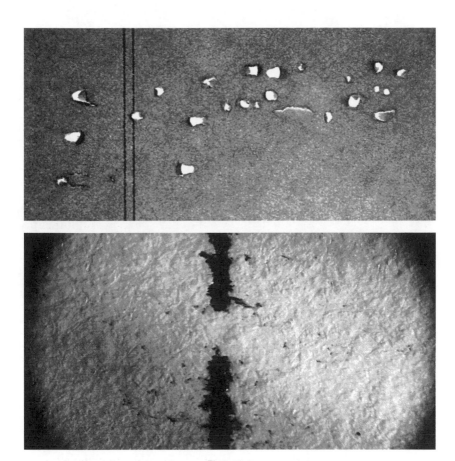

Figure 2.1

The upper frame of Figure 2.1 depicts staple holes photographed with transmitted light. That is, the document is placed on a light table with the light shining through the back of the document. The lower frame shows a break in a vertical line. This was the result of a defect in the printing process.

Latent Writing Tests

Latent writings cannot be seen with the naked eye. They are pen track depressions on the page that were made when entries were written on a previous page that was on top of the present page. For example, if a person is writing on page one of a tablet of paper, the pen pressure from page one transfers onto page two. At the moment page one is torn off and before anything is written on page two, page two carries the handwritten text from page one in the form of invisible impressions. The same thing may happen with any documents resting on top of each other, such as a stack of bond paper or a pile of envelopes. These invisible impressions can be made visible by various machines used by Questioned Document Examiners. This testing method is non-destructive, so it can be performed on the original record. Latent writing tests are often useful in examining anonymous documents (see Chapter 15) or medical records (see Chapter 10).

Handwriting Examinations

Admittedly, Questioned Document Examiners spend most of their time examining signatures and handwriting. During a handwriting comparison, the Document Examiner determines authenticity or fraud by comparing the questioned writing with known samples by suspects and victims. The distinctive handwriting habits of each person under consideration are compared with the questioned writing.

After the detailed analysis is concluded, the Document Examiner renders his professional opinion. If he is subpoenaed to court, he goes to assist the jury as tryers of fact under the Federal Rules of Evidence 702. If you want to read more about the examination of signatures, Appendix B contains a technical paper on the subject presented to the American Academy of Forensic Science, Questioned Document Section.

The most important element of handwriting analysis is an individual's signature. As we saw in Chapter 1, a signature is often forged in various ways on countless types of documents. The next chapter will discuss signatures in detail to teach you how to safeguard this important key to your identity.

THREE

THE POWER OF THE PEN

The Strength of Signatures on Documents

Personal as well as political realities have been fashioned by signatures on paper. Our relationships to family and associates, as well as countries' relationships to one another, are "sealed" by the use of signatures on important documents. By the stroke of pens, boundaries have been set, vast lands and even countries have been exchanged, fortunes have been transferred, treaties and laws have been established—all leading to the realities in which we travel, trade, and live out our lives in relationship to one another.

In fact, every major personal event of your life is attested to by a signature. A doctor signed your birth certificate, thus establishing your rights and privileges as a U.S. citizen. You entered school on the strength of a form that included a signature. Your high school and college diplomas are ratified with signatures. The purchase agreements for your car and house were bound with signatures, and your marriage was ratified by a license that bears an official's signature. Your business was established by "doing business as" ("Fictitious Business Name") statements, leases, and loans that were all secured by signatures. In fact, the rest of your life events, up to and including your death and burial, will be attested to by signature-bearing documents.

If at this very moment someone were to take away all of the documents and records that attest to your life events, then officially, you would not exist. You would have no rights, no privileges, no property, and formally, no relationships. Your life events may be distorted and your possessions taken away by someone's forging, counterfeiting, or otherwise altering these important documents.

A Piece of History

On the morning of September 2, 1945, on the deck of the *U.S.S. Missouri* in Tokyo Bay, the Japanese envoy's Foreign Minister Mamoru Shigemitsu and General Yoshijiro Umezu signed their names on the official Instrument of Surrender, prepared by the War Department and approved by President Truman. Afterward, Gen. Douglas MacArthur, Commander in the Southwest Pacific and Supreme Commander for the Allied Powers, also signed.

Figure 3.1

Figure 3.1 depicts the signing of the Official Instrument of Surrender on the deck of the U.S.S. Missouri *in Tokyo Bay.*

This document set out in eight short paragraphs the complete capitulation of Japan to the Allied Powers. After five years of human loss,

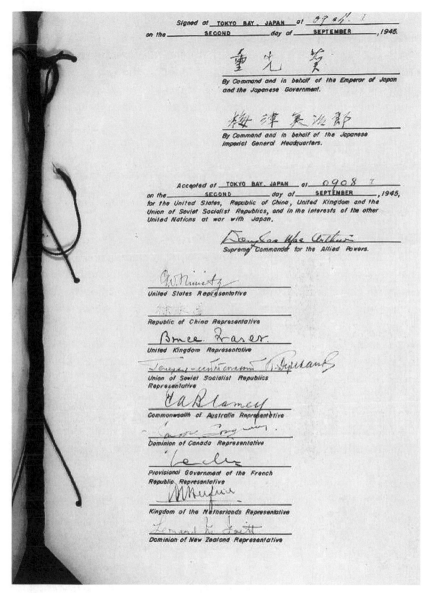

Figure 3.2

Figure 3.2 is a copy of the signature page of the Official Instrument of Surren-der. The signatures on this page restored order and peace to the then-torn and tattered world.

this single event marked the formal ending of hostilities in the Pacific and the termination of World War II. On that day, world reality changed, and millions of people could return to their homes and resume their normal lives. The Declaration of Independence, the U.S. Constitution, and all the other historic documents that created our great country were legitimately signed by recognized authorities. What power lies in the strength of signatures!

But all documents—whether they attest the birth of our country or the birth of an individual—are subject to forgery, counterfeiting, and alteration. It is essential, therefore, to understand how a true signature is formed—and how it can be forged—so as to learn ways to "forgeproof" your own signature.

The Anatomy of a Signature

When each of us was taught how to write in grade school, the teacher trained us to reproduce the letters of the alphabet as they appeared on the charts on the classroom wall and in our writing workbooks. But after completing our rudimentary training in handwriting, we were then free to "personalize" our own hand by departing from the copybook forms taught in school. Over time we further incorporated additional distinctive handwriting characteristics into our writing repertoire, which now manifest themselves in our "adult hand" in different ways. They appear as the unique manner in which we construct our letters and in unique forms and distinctive connections between letters.

There are different reasons why we write our signatures the way we do. Much of it is simply our own personal preferences. My sons tell me that the "B" of my surname looks like an "S" inside a circle. The reason for that is simple. When I was in junior high school, I had a friend named John Dumont. I watched him write his name one time and noticed that he began his "D" with an overhand motion, as when one begins the first counter-clockwise movement to make a capital "S." After descending to the baseline, the stroke rose up over the top of the first stroke, then created a large oval to form the remainder of the "D." When I saw that, I thought it was cool, so I began to make my "B" in a similar fashion, and through the years I have stylized it to the point that it now looks like an "S" in a circle.

Whatever the reasons behind our personalizing of our signatures, the resulting product is a "pictorial image" that is a certain shape, height, width, and size. And even though we may have forgotten the reasons our signature looks the way it does, when a document is placed before us, in a rapid, habitual burst of action we generate yet another authentic rendition of our own true signature.

Before learning how to protect your own unique signature, you should first understand the most common ways that signatures are forged.

Four Common Signature Forgery Techniques

Simple forgeries are those in which the forger writes the name of someone else with no attempt to replicate the appearance of the victim's true signature. These are the obvious forgeries, and they sometimes even exhibit the misspelling of the name! Let's say you were traveling with someone and stopped at a gas station to fill up. You had to use the restroom, so you told your traveling companion, "Please sign my name on the credit card receipt." In this instance, your friend would simply write your name in his or her own hand without trying to imitate your true signature. Although in this situation there is no intent to commit fraud, the resulting signature is similar to that of a simple forgery. It is your written name, but in the handwriting habits of another person.

Simulated forgeries are those in which the forger copies the likeness of a model signature he has obtained from a previous letter, invoice, check, receipt, or any other document bearing a rendition of the victim's true signature. When he copies the signature from the model, the model may be positioned right next to the document being forged, or in some cases, the model can be from memory if the situation calls for the forger to sign the victim's name while other people are around. In these situations the forger attempts to duplicate the obvious features, that is, the pictorial likeness of the model signature. He may have carefully practiced the signature several times before writing the forgery.

Traced forgeries are produced by placing a model signature on a light table (with light shining through the source document from behind), and placing the document to be forged on top. The forger, able to see the path of the signature line from the model document underneath, follows the line of the model projected from behind as he traces the forgery on the document above. Traced forgeries usually look correct as to letter forms and letter proportions, but they lack fluency. That is, traced forgeries exhibit poor "line quality" and lack tapering in beginning and ending strokes. However, since they look pretty accurate upon a casual glance, they usually pass scrutiny. Keep in mind that a forger is not trying to fool the professional handwriting expert; he is just trying to fool a clerk or someone at the point of exchange.

Can you tell which of the two signatures below is the real signature and which one is the traced forgery?

| Figure 3.3 | Figure 3.4 |

Figure 3.3 shows a true signature and Figure 3.4 shows the forgery. The forgery in the right frame exhibits hesitation, blunt strokes, and even, heavy line pressure, rather than the tapering and fluency of the authentic signature in the left frame.

Cut-and-paste forgeries are created when authentic signatures are misused by means of photocopiers or computer scanners. Your true signature is copied from a document you actually signed, but then that copied signature is placed onto a different document you've never seen before. In these situations, the resulting signature is not really a "forgery" strictly speaking because your signature has just been "recycled." However, we will still call it a forgery for our purposes since this situation represents an unauthorized use of your true signature to fraudulent ends. This method of forgery is becoming more prevalent in today's high-tech age with the advancement in quality of computer scanners and photocopying machines. Read more about such forgery in Chapter 14.

If you are interested in learning more about forgery detection principles, you can read a technical paper I presented to the American Academy of Forensic Sciences meeting in 1999 titled "Handwriting Identification: Formula for Authenticity." This brief paper can be found in Appendix B.

"Forgeproofing" Your Signature

Now that you understand how signatures are forged, there are several things you can do to prevent the misuse of your signature. First, don't make an abbreviated signature using only the initials of your name. As a rule of thumb, the fewer characters in a signature, the easier it is for the forger to succeed in producing the likeness of your written name, and the more difficult it will be for a questioned document expert to demonstrate that the signature is forged rather than authentic.

If you have been using an abbreviated signature, it is high time you started using most of the characters of both your given and surnames. I say "most" because if some of your characters become swallowed up in provocative flourishes and intricate and unique constructions and forms, then that can be advantageous, because a second rule of thumb is that intricate, stylized signatures provide the greatest deterrence to forgery.

Figure 3.5

Figure 3.5 depicts an "intricate, stylized" signature. Note the interesting constructions and artistic qualities. Only a microscope and experience can unravel the mysteries of such signatures.

Figure 3.5 is an example of a stylized signature, which usually cannot be easily deciphered. In fact, in some stylized signatures, perhaps fourteen characters can be represented by swirling circles or a series of jagged peaks.

Second, you should personalize your signature. The characters of your signature should not look like letters taken directly from the grade school handwriting charts that depict either the Palmer, the Zaner-Bloser, or the D'Nealian handwriting systems. By now, you should have injected some personal touches to the letters of your name with interesting constructions and forms and the use of connecting strokes.

Third, write your signature rapidly, letting the dynamics of your personal motor control add further distinctiveness to your written name. There are certain restrictions to what your hand, wrist, and forearm can do, and there are other motions that come naturally to your hand. Lately, I have noticed some strange but interesting-looking lower-case cursive "f"s being spawned by my hand. I do not tell my hand to make these; they just occur. These are distinctive and have identifying value, so I don't fight it. While I have consciously instructed my hand to make certain other constructions, it has obeyed in some ways, but it has demonstrated its resistance and independence in the creation of other forms. In any event, writing your signature rapidly guarantees uniqueness and distinctiveness, which is what you want to see in your authentic signatures.

In addition to developing a unique signature, there are many other practices you can follow to make it more difficult for forgers to reproduce or misuse your signature.

Use of Signature Stamps

In general, I don't recommend the use of a signature stamp. If someone were to abscond with your signature stamp, he or she could do a lot of damage to you personally and also to your business. If it is possible to do so, I advise taking the time to sign payroll checks. However, I do understand the need for signature stamps and automation in larger companies, where it would be too burdensome for one person to sign hundreds of checks. So if you have compelling reasons why you must continue to use stamps, I recommend the following:

Guidelines for the use of Signature Stamps:

1. Use only one signature stamp at a time.

2. When you begin using a signature stamp, note the date that you first put it in use, and also note the date when you retire it. When you first get it, stamp twenty samples of your signature stamp on a blank sheet. Write the date on the sheet of paper and file it in a safe place for future reference.

3. When you buy another signature stamp in the future, do not throw the old one away. It may be useful in dating a document if any issue ever arises concerning when a document may have been prepared. Lock the old stamp up in a

safe place, along with the original sample sheet that you made, and be sure to write down the date that you retired the old stamp.

4. Keep your active signature stamp locked up, with limited access by other personnel.

Use of Digital/Electronic Signatures ("e-signatures")

E-signatures have been gaining much hype in the news recently, and now they have gained legal acceptance. In June of 2000, the House of Representatives passed a bill to make e-signatures legally binding, and the Senate followed shortly with their hearty approval. Commerce Committee Chairman Thomas Bliley announced, "Electronic signatures and records will help grow the digital economy by giving American consumers greater confidence in their online business transactions."

Although I understand their enthusiasm, I also know that this step will open the door for perhaps the greatest wave of fraud yet. This new piece of legislation will allow consumers to buy a car, sign a mortgage, and accomplish all kinds of "e-business" using their computers. I can just see the scam artists drooling over this one. As for me, it will be some time before I entrust my personal signature to cyberspace. I will be watching for some time to see how this will play out. For the time being I would advise against the use of e-signatures, which will be discussed in detail in Chapter 14.

Use of Writing Implements

The best pens to use are ball-point pens or fountain pens, but do not use fiber-tip pens, broad-tip pens, or markers. Fiber-tip pens are among the best pens to use when forging a signature because they tend to conceal defects in the forgery, and they also conceal important details of authentic signatures. When you sign your name, you want all the distinctiveness of your natural handwriting to be seen in your authentic signature.

Remember, your signature is like a key to your front door. It unlocks the door and gives access to everything inside. Your signature authorizes the bank to release your money to another person. Your signature on a deed secures your ownership to land or property, and your signature on a trust or will tells the world how to distribute your estate when you are gone. Think about that—even after we are dead and gone, our signatures

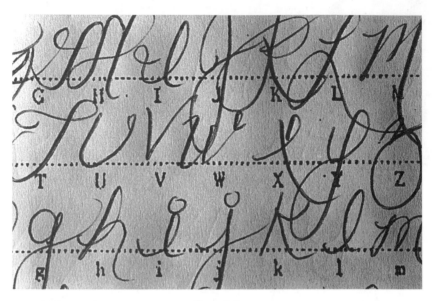

Figure 3.6

Although written with a ball-point pen, this handwriting sample exhibits the eloquence and tapering of fountain (nib) pens.

ensure the continued exercising of our desires and decisions. These signatures are powerful entities. Safeguard yours wisely. And before you jump on the "e-signature" bandwagon, be sure to read through Chapter 14.

Checklist: "Forgeproofing" Your Signature

1. Don't write an abbreviated signature. Use most of the characters of both your given and surnames.

2. Personalize your signature, letting your unique writing habits take over.

3. Write your signature rapidly.

4. Use ball-point or fountain pens. Do not use fiber-tip pens.

5. I don't recommend the use of signature stamps, but if you must use them, observe the guidelines above.

6. I don't yet recommend the use of "e-signatures."

FOUR

PREVENTING CONTRACT FRAUD

Preparing "Iron-clad" Contracts

The subject of this chapter might prompt you to ask, "Does Blanco think he's a lawyer?" No, I don't. I'm not offering "legal advice" as to how to properly prepare the content of a contract. Rather, I will show you how to add protective features to your contracts to safeguard them against the many subtle ways that "legally binding" contracts may become dismissed as contrived. I will also show you how to prevent bogus contracts and documents from gaining acceptance as legitimate and binding.

It is amazing to me that after great legal minds have consulted and agonized over a legal document, a creative criminal can still render such a document impotent. It is equally amazing how these creative scam artists can dupe entire juries and judges into believing that their bogus works of art are authentic and binding. By all means, use those brilliant legal minds to write your contracts, but protect that investment by adding the safeguards presented in this chapter. After first discussing the methods of fraud relative to contracts, I will describe preventative measures that will greatly reduce the risk of contract-related fraud.

Methods of Contract Fraud

Legitimate Contract Denial

People who have entered into a legitimate contractual agreement with you may attempt to break the contract by denying the authenticity of either their signatures or your signature on the valid contract. If they cannot explain away the authentic signatures, they may attack certain portions or certain pages of the contract. Let us now look at several forms of legitimate contract denial.

Signature Denial

One Sunday afternoon I was tinkering on my airplane in the hangar when I received a phone call from a man from India. He arrived to meet with me in Sacramento with a briefcase full of documents. It seemed his company needed to obtain proof that a vice president in their parent company in Italy had indeed signed an agreement some years earlier. The parent company was trying to renege on an old obligation by denying the authenticity of their representative's signature on this contract. As it turned out, the signature was authentic, and I sent this client home with a written report to that effect.

In a similar case, I recently worked a research and development contract out of Singapore. Three computer engineering consultants had entered into a consulting relationship with a company (my client) and later denied this relationship. After each of the three parties had signed the contract, they later denied doing so. My examination and report showed that they each did sign this document, and they were held to the agreement by their courts.

Although these matters were resolved favorably, I must point out the importance of having other signatures on file made by the people with whom you are doing business. Leading up to a contractual arrangement, you will usually receive letters, faxes, notes, and various communiqués. You should keep these documents in a file for future reference as resource signatures that could later be used should someone later deny his or her involvement with you.

In another case of signature denial, a developer had signed a Developer's Indemnity Agreement concerning a group of paper lots, and his signature on the agreement came into question. This developer was diagnosed as having Lou Gehrig's Disease. Those opposing the agreement used the developer's condition as an argument for his signature's being forged, taking the position that since he had Lou Gehrig's disease, he would not have been able to sign the document.

I traveled to a title company that had possession of the original document and was able to compare the questioned signature with many other samples of this man's signature of the same time period. I was able to determine that the signature was indeed authentic and that the subject had had sufficient motor skills during the time period in question to execute the authentic signature.

Substituted Page(s)

Another type of attack against authentic documents can sidestep signature issues by focusing on alleged substituted pages that change the terms of the contract. In this rendition of legitimate contract denial, the manipulators aren't trying to say that the entire contract is a fraud; they are just trying to argue away or change certain aspects of the agreement.

I recently took a trip to Pennsylvania to examine an important three-page document in such a case. The people who opposed the document kept trying to find problems with it so as to dismiss it as a fake. These attackers could not overcome the signature on page three, as their own expert had deemed it authentic, nor could they overcome evidence that the same typewriter was used to prepare all three pages. So they claimed instead that the first page of the agreement had indeed been typed by the same typewriter as pages two and three; however, they claimed that the typing on page one was made several years later and that the resulting text on page one substantially changed the agreement.

Fortunately, the original document was available for examination. Microscopic examination of the vertical pleading paper lines revealed that all three pages exhibited the same exact offset printing defect in the same location. These pages were companion pages as the result of a single print job at the printer when the document form stock was offset produced. This examination proved that all three of these sheets of paper were contemporaneous, as opposed to the argument that page one was from a ream of paper manufactured at a much later date. I provided photomicrographs (microscopic photographs) to the attorneys as proof.

Bogus Contract Enforcement

This type of contract fraud occurs when a contract that has been altered or tampered with—or created without the knowledge of one of the alleged parties—is presented as a legitimate and binding document. It too takes several forms, many of which involve forged or misused signatures.

Forged Signatures

One type of bogus contract enforcement occurs when a person's signature appears on a document that he or she never truly signed. In this instance, the signature is forged using one of the forgery methods discussed in Chapter 3. If this type of document emerges from an organization that you have already been doing some business with, they may have used your true signature from another document that you sent them in the normal course of business, such as a letter or a previous contract.

It is very common today for the unscrupulous to "recycle" authentic signatures by copying them from authentic contracts and "pasting" them onto bogus contracts. In these situations it is usually alleged by the proponents of the bogus document that they do not have the original document. They argue that you have the original and have destroyed it. This is a convenient argument, to be sure; however, there is a remedy in such situations. If, indeed, they have used a model signature of yours from a previous document that you sent them, and if you have a copy of that document, then it can be shown that the signature on the bogus document was taken from this previous authentic document.

Make sure that you keep copies of all documents that you send out that contain your signature. If there is a "cut and paste" forgery of your signature later, the first point of comparison would be with your copies of all documents that you have sent to them, since these would have provided a resource pool of model signatures—your signatures.

In one example of bogus contract enforcement, an employee forged his boss's name to an employment contract that forever assigned preferred stock in the amount of 15% to the employee "for consideration which has been received." The contract also guaranteed perpetual employment. This employee was trying to enforce this bogus contract, which, of course, the company owner had never agreed to or even seen.

In a different case, a child died in an apartment fire because the smoke detector, whose battery had expired, did not function to wake up the tenant in time to escape. At trial, the apartment owner offered a one-page "Smoke Detector Agreement" wherein the renter allegedly acknowledged her understanding that she was supposed to do a weekly test of the smoke detector and replace the battery if the detector did not function. However, in truth, the tenant had never signed any such document and had assumed that the smoke detector was powered by electricity rather than batteries. The landlord had forged the tenant's signature to this document in the hope of sidestepping any responsibility in this ugly situation.

A bogus contract or document may also emerge from a source that is unknown to you, who nevertheless claims that you have entered into some arrangement with him, her, or them. They produce a copy of a document, and you might even be convinced that the signature on it is one of your true signatures, but you know that you have never done any business with this company before. Remember that there are four kinds of forgeries and that there are different levels of skilled forgeries. Some forgeries may be so skilled as to fool even you, so you must always check your memory and your records to be sure that you really haven't done any business with this company before.

A word of caution is in order here: do not be one of those people who sign stacks of documents all at once without checking the actual text of the documents. Sometimes bogus documents are slipped into a stack of documents to be signed, and the unsuspecting person signs the document without reading it over. It does not wash well with the court to say, "Your honor, I never would have signed a contract like that." There have been many times that I have had to tell clients that they really did sign documents that they did not recall signing. In these cases they were just careless; however, there is another side to strange appearances of true signatures on documents.

Signature Epiphanies

A single man in Montana had owned and lived in a house for fifteen years. He married, and his new bride joined him in his home. However, they began to have problems in their marriage, and after two years they separated. During court proceedings the woman presented an Equity Purchase Agreement to the court. This document, which conveyed half of this man's property to her, seemed to have his true signature on it.

This was a miraculous appearance of a true signature on a bogus document. What had happened was that the creative young bride, who had possession of the house and all of the file cabinets, had found a document signed by the husband with a lot of blank room above the signature.

That is, he had signed this particular document way at the bottom, far below the last line of typed text. She had simply cut off the page at the bottommost portion of the existing text, but far above the signature. That left her enough room to type in a date and five lines of new text above the true signature.

So the man had truly signed the document—however, the original substance had been completely removed and a brand new text added! The substance of this new text was enough to convince the court to award the man's home to the woman. Another word of caution: Sign documents just below the text of the agreement, not way down at the bottom. I call this the "two inch rule"—never allow more than two inches of blank space between the last line of text and the top portion of your signature.

Substituted Page(s)

An owner of a restaurant sent documents to me for examination. He was having some problems with the State Board of Equalization, and he wanted me to examine a document submitted to the Board that bore his alleged signature. During my examination I noticed a problem with the third page of the Sales Purchase Contract. My client remembered signing a purchase contract and thought that this was his true signature on this particular page; however, the first two pages did not contain content that he had agreed to.

When I pointed out the inconsistencies of the copy quality and trash marks on the third page as opposed to the first and second pages, he realized that although the signature page was a true copy of an agreement that he had previously signed, pages one and two were brand-new pages that had been attached to the copy of the signature page.

Altered Contracts: The "Better and Improved" Contract Scam

In this type of scam, new ingredients are added to a preexisting authentic contract by the party making the changes for his own benefit. For example, a resurfacing company had agreed to resurface four tennis courts for a property management company. The resurfacing company prepared a typewritten proposal of what they agreed to do for a particular dollar amount. Later, when challenged as to the quality of their workmanship, they produced their copy of the contract. It now contained the added handwritten phrase "Patched areas peeling around edges" to argue that there was a pre-existing condition that resulted in premature cracking soon after they had resurfaced the tennis courts.

However, this handwritten phrase was not included on the property manager's original contract. By performing a solubility test of an area where some of the handwritten text intersected a dated rubber stamp impression, I was able to establish that the disputed handwritten entry was added after the work had been agreed to and paid for. This proved that the resurfacing company had altered the original agreement in their favor.

The truth needs your help.

Being "right" is not enough. In our court systems these days, the truth does not come to light on its own; it needs help. Truth needs to be accompanied by proof, and that proof needs to be demonstrated in a practical, clear, and relevant way so that it makes sense and is convincing. This cannot be accomplished if you have been losing, throwing away, or destroying documents, whether they are contracts, invoices, or receipts.

Many unsuspecting souls have been pinched by not adhering to this guideline. If your opponent in a matter has documentation that is contrived, and you have nothing but your memory and good name to present, then it is your word against his evidence. Your opponent will more than likely prevail if he enters a hearing or courtroom with documentation, albeit falsified documentation, and you enter with only your story or a supporting witness. With this in mind, always try to keep original documents for your own files whenever possible; give copies away. Original documents are your best defense when the veracity of any document is later attacked.

Remedies to Contract Fraud

These are precautionary measures you can take to greatly reduce the chance of contract fraud being committed against you:

Don't sign uncompleted forms.

Don't sign documents "in blank"—that is to say, don't sign a pre-printed form that has not yet been filled out. Sign only documents with all of the terms and information completely filled out. There was a large operation developer who had been doing a lot of business with a certain bank and had entered into a trusting relationship with one particular loan officer. After discussing the details of a new loan, this loan officer convinced the developer to sign two promissory note forms "in blank," even though no terms or amounts had yet been typed into the blank spaces. The reason the loan officer gave for wanting signatures on two promissory notes was that the second form would be used in case there was an error while typing up the first one. So this trusting developer signed these two notes.

At first, everything went as planned. The developer received fifteen million dollars for his project, and he began making the agreed payments on the loan. But sometime later he was contacted by a different department of this bank and asked why payments were not being made on a second loan. Of course, the developer denied any knowledge of this second loan, whereupon the bank proceeded to place liens against his heavy equipment as collateral against this second note for twenty million dollars! This developer discovered that taking on a large bank in court can be a daunting task—a task, in this case, that could have been avoided had the developer not been so trusting

The carbon film laid down by the typewriter ribbon (Figure 4.1 at right) was removed from the intersecting area of the typed letter "E" at the middle horizontal bar. The upper picture was taken before anything was done to the document, and the lower frame was taken after the portion of carbon film had been removed. Permission was obtained from the judge to remove a small portion of the carbon typing ribbon to show what was underneath the typing.

If only the whiteness of the paper had been revealed under the carbon film, that would mean that the document had been signed after it was typed. Therefore the argument would be that the developer had knowledge of what he had signed. In Figure 4.1, however, the lower frame shows that instead of the whiteness of the paper, the ink from the pen was observed when the carbon film was removed. This showed that the document was indeed signed in blank and that the information had been typed over the signature sometime after it was signed.

Sign all pages of important documents.

When signing contracts, it is best to have each party sign on each page, as pages can easily be substituted. I have signed court documents in Mexico twice recently, and I like what they do. They have each person sign each and every page of the pertinent series of documents before the parties leave. I noticed that this takes only an additional five minutes or so. It is an excellent practice.

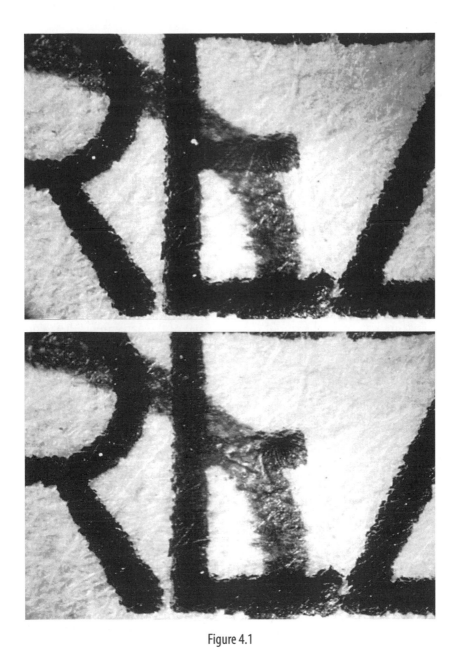

Figure 4.1

Figure 4.1 depicts a photomicrograph of an intersecting area where the signature line passes over the typed character "E."

Read contracts before signing them.

This might sound obvious, but you would be surprised at how many people sign documents without actually reading them. The truth of the matter is that if they had read certain contracts and understood the conditions, they would never have signed those agreements! Many times after examining a case, I have had to tell the person who brought me the documents that his or her signature is indeed authentic. If the client says, "I never would have signed a document such as that," I respond with questions such as, "Do you have a secretary that brings you stacks of papers to sign all at once?" and "Have you ever signed any documents 'in blank'?" Remember: do not be one of those people who signs stacks of documents all at once without checking the actual text of the documents.

Leave your invisible link.

Here is a handy intrepid feature you can easily add that will link the signature page (last page) with the first page of a multi-page contract. When you are satisfied with the contract and are ready to sign, fold the signature page over the top of the first page of the agreement, then sign your name with a good healthy dose of pen pressure. By so doing you will leave an invisible impression of your signature indented into the first page.

This way, if your signature page is ever removed from the agreement at hand and attached to a different contract, the absence of your indented link on page one will be part of your argument against this bogus agreement. Any Questioned Document Examiner could process the original of page one to show whether or not your signature imprint is present. Of course, your testimony would have to be that you began such a practice with all of your documents on a certain date.

Initial all handwritten changes or corrections to contracts.

Initial any changes any of the parties make to documents you sign. If a typed contract, for example, has been legitimately corrected or changed by handwritten interlineation, then you should initial the corrections. You should also make sure that every other party to the document also initials the changes. If a numeric amount has been changed, whether by hand or by machine, all the parties to the contract should initial the change.

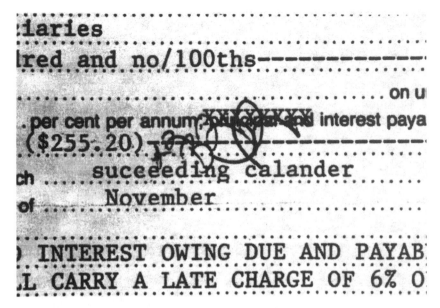

Figure 4.2

Three different people have initialed the changed typewritten numeric amount of "$255.20." The original entry was whited out and then typed over.

Notarize important contracts.

Have the document notarized by the parties. Notaries will come to your location if you set up a meeting with them ahead of time, and a notary can notarize just about any document (See Glossary, p. 215). This adds an extra avenue of proof when preparing those important documents because later, the notary can be contacted as a witness to identify the parties that signed the document. He or she will also have the notarial journal, which has a record of how the notary identified the signers and which will also contain sample signatures by the principles to the contract.

Of course, there have been instances in my experience in which I have known notaries to lie or to lose important documents they were supposed to keep (like their notarial journal), as well as other cases in which notary stamps have been counterfeited. However, cases such as these are indeed the exceptions rather than the rule. Nearly all notaries are professional and ethical people, and involving them adds an extra touch of professionalism, security, and dignity to your important contracts.

Number pages of contracts.

It is expedient to number, title, and date each page of any contracts that exceed one page. That makes it more difficult for the person to duplicate the font size, typestyle, and locations of all of the writings on the pages.

Use systematic spacing.

When preparing contracts, make sure there are no large gaps or spaces between paragraphs so as to make it difficult for someone to add lines of text that would modify the contract. Make sure the line spacing, paragraph spacing, margins, and other formatting considerations are consistent throughout.

Retain documents or copies.

Keep copies of all documents you send out and receive, whether they be important contracts or simple invoices or faxes. As computer archiving becomes more popular, just realize that when you destroy documents after you have scanned or otherwise digitized them, you have destroyed your most effective evidence in resolving disputes.

Checklist: General Practices Concerning Contracts

1. Keep copies of signatures of the people with whom you are in business or negotiating for business.

2. Copy every document you send out that contains your signature.

3. Do not sign stacks of documents without reading them.

4. The preparation of a will is a little different than the preparation of everyday contracts. After reviewing the following guidelines in this chapter, you should also observe the additional recommendations addressed in Chapter 12 on Probate Fraud.

Checklist: Before Signing Contracts and Other Important Documents

1. Make sure you are satisfied as to all of the terms of the con-

tract. That means you have to actually read it thoroughly and thoughtfully!

2. Ensure that all of the pages are numbered, titled, and dated.

3. Check the formatting: Is there consistency in paragraph indentations, margins, and font? If the document appears bogus to start with, have it redone.

4. Make sure that when you enter into a contract you are not intoxicated, medicated, or going through emotional turmoil such as a divorce. Many a person has tried to get out of a legally binding contract by saying, "I was intoxicated when I signed it."

5. Avoid signing contracts at business luncheons or dinners where you have been drinking alcoholic beverages.

Checklist: During the Signing of Contracts and Other Important Documents

1. Remember the two-inch rule. Sign just below the text of the agreement, and don't leave more than two inches of blank space between the last line of text and the top portion of your signature.

2. Do not sign forms "in blank"—that is, forms that have not been completely and properly filled out, whether by hand or by a typewriter or computer printer.

3. Use a blue ball-point pen or fountain pen. The color blue makes it obvious right away that the document is a signed original (with the exception of cut-and-paste forgeries using color printers).

4. Use the same pen for all signatures, initials, and handwritten entries you make for that particular contract.

5. If possible, sign all of the pages of the contract, or at least initial and date all pages of the contract.

6. Leave your invisible link. Before signing on the last page,

the signature page, turn that page over so that it is on top of the first page of the agreement. Then sign with a healthy dose of pen pressure.

7. Be sure that you and all the other principals to a contract initial any changes that are to be made.

8. Notarize the contract if appropriate.

9. Take time to ensure that the contract is "signed, sealed, and delivered" properly before leaving the meeting. Don't leave the meeting expecting others to sign or initial changes after you are gone.

Checklist: After Signing Contracts and Other Important Documents

1. Make and file copies of all contracts you sign. These will provide the basis for analysis regarding incidents of bogus contract enforcement should these signatures of yours be misused on bogus documents in the future.

2. Keep all documents you receive from others. These will provide the basis for analysis regarding legitimate contract denial should the other party try to get out of a good contract in the future.

3. Keep the originals whenever you can.

4. Request a copy of the computer file that prepared the contract. If you prepared it yourself, you can simply save a copy to a floppy disk and put the disk with the contract. The importance of this practice will be discussed in detail in Chapter 14.

ACCOUNTING AND GENERAL BUSINESS PRACTICES

Everyday Protection Against Potential Fraud

Many methods for protecting yourself and your business from fraud simply require good old common sense. Others involve more complex issues of which you may not be aware. This chapter offers some examples of business-related scams and frauds. It also conveys practical advice that you can implement to help deter fraud in many different types of businesses.

"Fraudproof" Your Accounting Practices

Beware of embezzlement schemes.

Embezzlement can be defined as "taking fraudulently in violation of a trust." Some of the simpler forms of embezzlement involve employees' stealing company checks and then forging them, making the checks payable to themselves and claiming that the company owed them those funds. In a similar type of scam, I worked a case in which a woman stole fifteen checks while she was employed by an insurance company. She forged these checks and deposited them to a fictitious account, which she soon liquidated. These checks totaled over $100,000.

In another version of this scam, the bookkeeper takes one of your company checks and makes it payable to a fictitious company. The book-keeper has already had an accomplice set up a fictitious business account in the phony company name that appears as payee on the check in question. Of course, the address shown on the signature card at the bank is bogus, occupying the space between two legitimate addresses. The bookkeeper then gives the check to the accomplice, who cashes it at the bank that has the fictitious account. Your bookkeeper could also simply deposit such forged checks at the ATM or night drop, then return a few days later to cash out the account by several draws against the ATM machine.

This is a profitable scam for the bookkeeper because there is certainly plausible deniability and low risk. A $10,000 check could easily be liquidated within a few weeks—if not sooner, depending on the bank—and you would not be aware of it until the damage was already done. In fact, skilled bookkeepers can cook the books so well that a year could go by before the embezzled money would be noticed. In some cases, losses could even be disguised so cleverly that the company owner would never notice at all.

There are simple precautions that you can take against such embezzlement schemes. My late father used to be the head accountant for the Academy of Arts and Motion Pictures, as well as Comptroller for Carter Hawley Hale Stores, Inc., and troubleshooter for various other large institutions. He told me that there is an old accounting rule for companies that many seem to ignore today: you should not have the same person handling both disbursements and revenue. That is, the person who logs in your company's income should not be the person who pays the company bills. In large corporations these divisions are rather natural; however, in medium-size to smaller companies, the same person may often handle both revenue as well as disbursements.

When only one person handles both revenue and disbursements, this same person skimming off money on the disbursement side can cover his tracks on the revenue side. Two different persons, who are not best friends, should be in charge of these sides of your company's accounting departments so as to guarantee that you don't get pinched at either end of the equation. This is an obvious safeguard which your company should practice, if it is not already doing so. Further, all of your company accounts should be reconciled at least every month. The earlier you notice that something is going wrong, the greater chance you will have of remedying the problem and minimizing your losses.

It is a good idea to have the bank mail original, canceled company checks and monthly statements to a different address than that used by the person(s) authorized to disburse funds. I recommend that the business owner or manager have the canceled checks mailed to his or her home address or a different business P.O. Box, then take a few minutes each month to review each check.

Look for obvious fraud, such as checks made payable to employees from an account not used for payroll. Look more closely periodically to ensure that each check is made payable to a legitimate business account and that it matches both the payee and the amount listed in the account ledger. If it is the routine policy of management to take physical possession of the account ledger monthly and compare the returned checks, it is very unlikely that fraudulent accounting schemes will be perpetrated against you.

Bogus Invoicing Scams

Bookkeepers should always check invoices against orders to make sure that they are paying for something that was actually ordered by some one in your company. Remember, there are scams out there in which bogus invoices are sent to your company as though they are items that are routinely paid.

One type of bogus invoice scam can take the form of embezzlement by an employee of your company. This scam can be perpetrated using past recycled invoices or new fabricated invoices that bear the likeness of authorized signatures, which could be cut-and-paste forgeries or just handwritten "simple" forgeries. The bookkeeper then writes a company check to pay for the invoiced item and negotiates the check through a dummy bank account that has been set up for this purpose. The shady bookkeeper then pockets the money and covers his or her paper trail by any number of methods.

In external occurrences of invoicing scams, a vendor with whom you have done previous business may use a past authentic invoice that already bears a true rendition of your signature. The creator of the new, bogus invoice would simply use white-out to change the date, the items ordered, and the amounts.

A case in point: A large utilities company contracted out landscaping work to be done at approximately thirty company locations. Previous legitimate work orders were "cleaned up" by the shady vendor, who used white-out and then retyped dates, internal control numbers, descriptions of work performed, and billing amount totals. At the bottom of the work order, the company officials' signatures were forged. Numerous work orders were included on invoices that were mailed to the utility company. These invoices were paid until discrepancies were noted during a general audit.

Another method for creating bogus invoices is to use a cut-and-paste forgery of your signature. That is, the outside vendor would prepare a new invoice to his liking, then use a model signature of yours copied from a previous authentic invoice that you truly did sign. He would attach your signature via computer scanning technology or by using a photocopy machine. Your bookkeeper might pay these invoices if he or she were not paying attention to the big picture.

You may also receive bogus billings for non-received, unrequested, or inferior goods and services. This scam is similar to the bogus-invoice scam, except that these billings are pulled out of thin air. A scam now being perpetrated against many companies, including my own, involves billings for "Yellow Pages" advertising. I have actually received these bogus billings, and they do appear to be legitimate. The company that billed me would probably argue that such billings were not "bogus" because the customer would receive a listing in their directory. However, the billing itself is extremely misleading, as it presents itself as a rebilling for the continuation of existing service. I just happened to compare this billing with my previous year's order, and I realized that this invoice was really a new invoice from a directory I had never previously done business with nor contacted.

It may be that you receive goods or services that you never ordered, or you may receive inferior products, or you may receive nothing at all after paying certain invoices. The point is, these are invoices for goods or services that were never intentionally ordered by anyone from your company. If your bookkeepers are not alert, they could innocently pay these invoices.

A further complication can occur if employees responsible for paying bills in your company have other major responsibilities in addition to handling accounts payable. Furthermore, nearly half of all companies do not require a second approval before billings are paid. This is why bogus bills for goods and services end up getting paid unwittingly.

Businesses nationwide are scammed for hundreds of millions of dollars each year through phony invoicing schemes. It is important that your bookkeepers always compare invoices against orders or requests made for the goods and services being invoiced. For this reason, it is good to always add an internal authorization number for goods and services being ordered. That way, when the invoice does arrive, the bookkeeper can compare the invoice against the authorization number or request, just to be sure that he or she is paying for something that someone in your company really did order. Although this may add another step to your bookkeeping system, crooks rely on inattention to such detail and other careless bookkeeping practices to pull off their schemes.

The best way to protect your company against phony invoice scams is by making your entire disbursements staff aware of such potential stings, as well as by putting preventative measures in place. If a billing is suspected of being fraudulent, bookkeepers should do the following:

1. Examine each bill carefully. Check files for a pending order or contract to ensure that the mailing relates to advertising, merchandise, or services that have been legitimately ordered.

2. If an invoice is determined to be bogus, photocopy it and distribute it to accounts payable staff.

3. Notify the local postal inspector. The United States Postal Service works to stop fraudulent and misleading solicitations, and they want to be informed.

Phone Solicitations

Exercise caution when making purchases over the phone in response to a phone solicitation unless you have a history with the supplier or vendor. Scammers sometimes obtain the names of your business employees and assert that these persons have placed orders on behalf of your business in the past. Instruct your bookkeepers to verify the order with the person by whom it was allegedly placed.

Ask for verification of offers in writing. If a caller makes an offer that interests you regarding the provision of goods or services, request that the offer be made in writing and forwarded to you for review. Be suspicious if the caller refuses to forward this information to you or to otherwise provide references.

Merchandise Return Scams

In addition to bookkeeping and invoice embezzlement schemes, there are other types of embezzlement that get more creative and complicated. An employee for a home building supply store filled out over 150 refund/merchandise credit vouchers and made fictitious entries on them, making up customer names and addresses and writing in expensive store items which had supposedly been returned. Since the vouchers indicated that the sale items had been paid for in cash, the employee put these cash amounts in his pocket. Working alone at the returns counter, this industrious embezzler was able to misappropriate around $100,000 with his simple scheme.

To prevent this scam, you should ensure that returned items go back on the store inventory, which should then balance with all merchandise credit vouchers. If you balance these weekly (daily is best), you will have a good handle on company cash receipts and inventory and will thereby protect yourself against such embezzlements.

Another merchandise return scam involves the use of counterfeited cash register receipts. Although such a scam might seem insignificant, one company lost $60,000 on this type of scheme. A man went into a home-improvement store (name not specified to protect the embarrassed) and purchased a wall-mount air conditioning unit for about $1,000. This initial, legitimate purchase was made with cash. The original cash register receipt given to the scam artist was one of those blue dot-matrix printed receipts, which he then color-copied numerous times. He gave copies to his cohorts, who worked as a team over a period of several weeks, performing the following scam against three different locations of these stores.

The crook would enter the store, go back to the display of air conditioners, and place on a flat roller a unit similar to the one previously purchased. He then worked his way up to the returns desk, which was located near the entrance. While the employee at the return desk was distracted, the scammer positioned himself so as to appear to be just entering the store with the unit when he approached the desk. He then explained to the returns clerk that he was returning the item because it did not meet his needs for some reason. He then produced the counterfeit receipt, which bore the same stock number. The clerk would fill out a refund slip and return the $1,000 cash to the crook, as that was the original method of payment shown on the receipt.

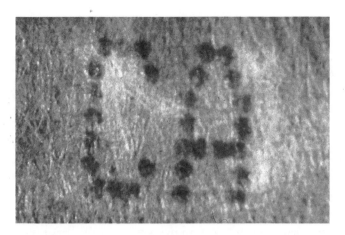

Figure 5.1

Photomicrograph of the authentic cash register receipt. Notice the round dots that make up the characters "CA." These round dots are also blue and usually show impact into the paper since they are printed by a 9-pin dot matrix printer.

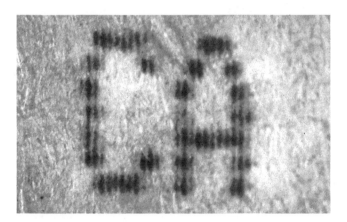

Figure 5.2

Photomicrograph of the counterfeited cash register receipt. Notice the vertical dash marks that demonstrate the color copier's interpretation of the original round dots of the authentic receipt. Further, these lines exhibit the colors cyan and magenta in close proximity to one another to give the illusion of the color blue to the unaided eye.

These creative thieves continued working this scam for several weeks—careful not to be too obvious—to the tune of $60,000 in losses against this chain of stores. These losses could even have been much higher, except that when the accounting department noticed a discrepancy between stock and revenue, an investigation ensued and the scam was uncovered.

This type of scam points out the need to balance inventory against revenue frequently. It also demonstrates the importance of having attentive people at the returns counter who have been briefed on the methods of such scams. Also, it would be beneficial to educate the returns desk staff on the details of your register receipts. They should recognize the standard size and formatting, the type of paper, the kind of mechanical typing (whether it is thermal, dot-matrix or some other process), and the information that should appear on the receipts. A one-hour staff meeting during which you hand out loupes and mag lights (see Chapter 6) and instruct your employees on examining the details of your receipts would go a long way toward staving off counterfeit receipt fraud against your business.

Preparing Company Checks

If you are unfamiliar with check terminology, then you may want to review Chapter 6, which explains the anatomy of checks. Since there are so many ways to alter a check, there are several things you should do to prevent their misuse.

Take precautions against legitimate checks being "raised."

When filling out checks, you should start entries in the dollar amount box, on the payee line, and on the written amount line from the far left. These are the lines that can be altered by changing the payee or raising the amounts. The following two figures show the right way (Figure 5.3) and the wrong way (Figure 5.4) to fill out a check.

Figure 5.4 demonstrates the wrong way to fill out a check. In figure 5.4 (right) the dollar amount and legal amount have been innocently placed in the middle of the lines. The following figure, Figure 5.5 (page 54), shows what a resourceful con artist can do with a check that has not been properly filled out. He can simply write in a few numbers to the left of the dollar amount entry and a few words to the left of the legal amount entry to raise the check. This allows him to use your good check without forging your name, and he can raise the amount of the check substantially while putting very little of his own handwriting on the check.

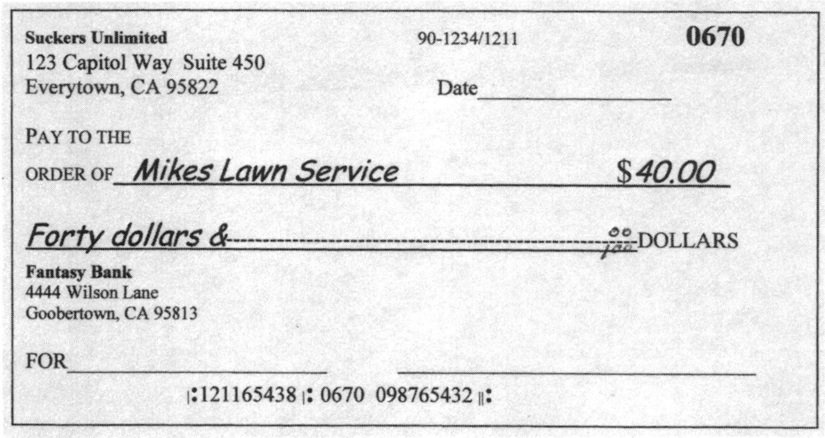

```
Suckers Unlimited                    90-1234/1211              0670
123 Capitol Way  Suite 450
Everytown, CA 95822                  Date_____

PAY TO THE
ORDER OF  Mikes Lawn Service                    $40.00

Forty dollars &---------------------------°°⁄₁₀₀DOLLARS
Fantasy Bank
4444 Wilson Lane
Goobertown, CA 95813

FOR_____    _____
        |:121165438 |: 0670  098765432 ||:
```

Figure 5.3

Figure 5.3 shows the correct way to fill out a check. The payee, the dollar amount, and the written amount entries are positioned to the far left.

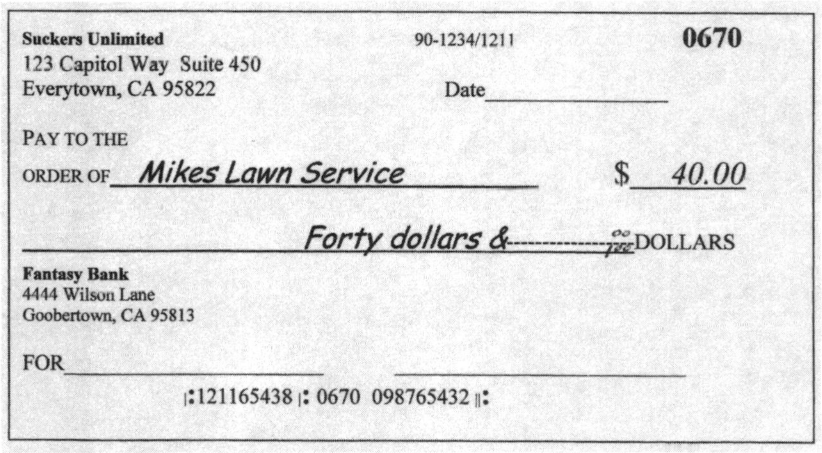

```
Suckers Unlimited                    90-1234/1211              0670
123 Capitol Way  Suite 450
Everytown, CA 95822                  Date_____

PAY TO THE
ORDER OF  Mikes Lawn Service            $   40.00

_____  Forty dollars &----------°°⁄₁₀₀DOLLARS
Fantasy Bank
4444 Wilson Lane
Goobertown, CA 95813

FOR_____    _____
        |:121165438 |: 0670  098765432 ||:
```

Figure 5.4

In Figure 5.4 the check writer has offered an opportunity to a scam artist or an unethical vendor to alter or raise this check.

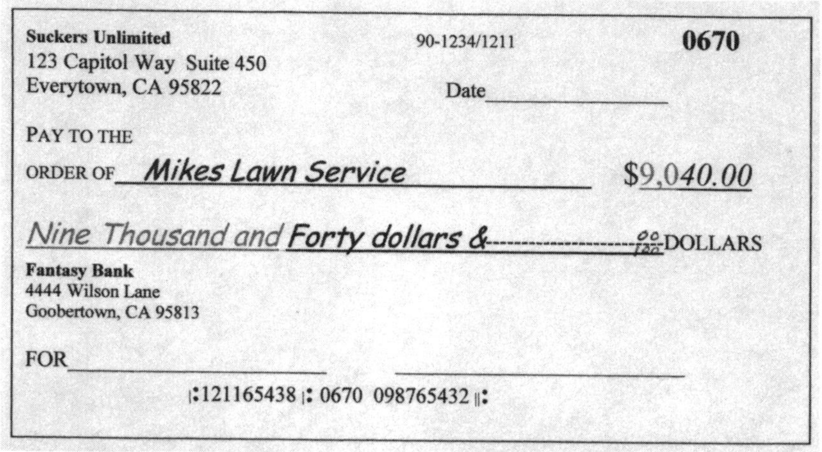

Figure 5.5

Figure 5.5 depicts how a person can "raise" the original amount of your authentic check.

In the previous three figures we see how Mike of Mike's Lawn Service has absconded with more money than he was supposed to have. True, you did write him a check—but for much less than he took.

We have already seen in Chapter 1 what can happen to a check when a crook intercepts it and then creatively changes the payee name. To make it more difficult for a forger to alter the payee, make sure you write out a complete payee name. Avoid using abbreviations or simply writing "Cash."

If your personal or business checks have been forged or raised, you should first fill out a police report or phone in an incident report, and get a report number from the police.

Then go to your bank and fill out affidavits of forgery for each item, making sure to list all checks that have been forged. In this situation, the bank now must reimburse your account for the lost funds since it accepted a check that was not truly signed by you. However, the bank now has the right to investigate and pursue you if they believe that you are lying about your checks being forged. Many people who run out of money will write non-sufficient-fund checks, then later claim that their checkbook was stolen and these checks were forged.

Destroy old deposit slips.

When you run out of checks and add new checks in your checkbook, don't just throw away the old deposit slips. These can legitimately be used as checks by simply writing "This is a Check" on the deposit slip. You should shred them, or at least tear them up and properly dispose of them. Also, properly dispose of old checks that you do not intend to use.

Time Card Schemes

One easy way that employees can take money from your company is simply by raising the time amounts on their time cards if they are kept by hand. This is like a slow leak in a pool: you don't notice the leak for awhile, and it's hard to find. If this kind of fraud continues over time, you may start to wonder where your profits are going. Detection is difficult because all of your books will balance, giving you an unrealistic appraisal of your company's performance.

I had a case in the state of Washington in which this type of fraud occurred. When no one was looking, some of the employees in this company would take their time cards and raise the numbers for the week by alteration. It's very easy to turn a "6" into an "8," for example, or a "1" into a "7" or "9." Another twist to this scheme occurs when working employees fill in time values for other employees who were not working on those particular days.

Yet another time card scam occurs when a temporary employee uses a copy of a legitimate time card, which bears the approving signature of a supervisor, and changes the dates, then submits the cards to the temp agency as additional periods worked. The distance between the employer's HR department and the temp agency creates a natural lag in communication, allowing this scam to go on undetected for quite some time. When dealing with a temp agency, consider faxing copies of approved time cards to the temporary agency, to be followed by delivery of the original via routing channels. Any differences between the original and the faxed copies will expose fraud quickly.

It is best to use a mechanical time card machine that automatically stamps the dates and times. You shouldn't trust employees to fill in their time cards by hand, as this offers them too great a temptation to commit fraud against you. The machine and cards should be kept in a busy but controlled location, so that employees can't make changes when no one is looking. After the time cards are processed, business owners should keep all original copies locked up in a safe place with limited access to employees. Employers should not get rid of originals, as they are their best evidence should any disputes arise down the road.

Checklist: Accounting Do's and Don'ts

1. Golden Rule: Do not let the accountant or bookkeeper who handles revenue or opens the mail also handle disbursements.

2. Do reconcile your accounts at least monthly.

3. Do have your bank mail your returned company checks and your monthly statements to an address inaccessible to your accounting personnel. The owner or manager should

    a) Review such checks and statements monthly to watch for fraud.
    b) Compare checks to the company ledger. Make certain that payees on check match payees shown on the ledger.
    c) Confirm that the payees and amounts on checks are consistent and believable with your company's practice.

4. Do not let the returns counter employees be solo performers. Team them up.

5. Do balance inventory with revenue as well as with disbursements.

6. Do consider adding an internal authorization number for goods and services being ordered.

7. Do have accounts payable personnel check invoices against orders to make sure they are paying for what your company has really ordered.

8. Do instruct your bookkeepers to verify phone orders with the person by whom they were allegedly placed.

9. Do fill checks out starting at the far left. Write out the complete payee name; avoid using abbreviations or writing "cash."

10. Do shred or tear up old deposit slips and old unused checks.

11. Do use a mechanical time card machine, placed in a busy but controlled location.

General Office Procedures

Although safeguarding your accounting procedures will prevent many potential types of fraud against your business, there are other office procedures that business owners and managers should also follow to further protect their companies.

Secure your private office.

Company owners, managers, and accounting staff should take care to safeguard their offices when leaving to attend a meeting, go to lunch, or go home for the evening. Remove important documents from the top of your desk, and secure them in locked file cabinets. Lock up your desk, your office windows, and your doors as well. Restrict the number of sets of keys to your office, and consider well who should be given sets of keys.

A new restaurant owner learned about the importance of securing his office the hard way. The city council had encouraged this restaurant owner to hire local people, and he had complied. After the first month of business, the restaurant owner noticed that many checks were missing from his business checkbook. The owner had left the business checkbook out, and one of the employees had removed several checks from the back of the checkbook so that it would take time for the owner to notice they were missing. The employee then enlisted the help of her partners in crime, filling out and passing these forged checks to local banks, merchants, and check cashing stores.

Since it took awhile for the owner to notice that checks were missing, he did not at first suspect that anything was wrong. Also, since bank statements with which to reconcile a checkbook ledger are issued only once a month, these forgers had at least a month's head start. A month's time can leave a cold trail for investigators. The lessons to be learned are clear: don't leave your checkbook out where employees or passersby may help themselves to your blank checks; and secure your office when you are away.

Handle mail with caution.

Don't put your outgoing mail in a common location where passersby may put their hands in and remove mail, and don't have your mail delivered to you at a location accessible to the public. If you run a small business out of your home, this also applies to personal mailboxes that are on the front porch or on the street. There are at least two things that scam artists can do with your incoming or outgoing mail.

When you put mail out after writing accounts-payable checks, crooks can intercept these checks, photocopy them (to remember what your signature is supposed to look like), then wash them with chemicals to remove the information that you wrote on the checks. They then fill out the checks with new payees, forge your signature, and deposit them into bogus accounts. In a couple of days, they cash out these holding accounts, then vanish before you ever find out that your accounts payable have not reached their intended destinations.

Another thing fraud artists can do is simply to take one of your checks and obtain your bank branch information and your personal account information, then use any number of computer programs to print out new checks, using one of their alias names and your good account number. The personalized information on these checks will coincide with the crook's phony driver's license, so everything will appear legitimate to those accepting these hybrid checks. These crooks will be able to pass these checks, and they will clear the bank because there is indeed money in these accounts—your money!

In addition to stealing your outgoing mail, creative scammers also like to intercept your incoming mail and look for the juicy stuff. They take those credit offers we are bombarded with, fill them out, and forge your name, but they then note an address change so that the new credit cards go to their mail drop. When the cards arrive, they begin charging items or taking cash advances until they have maxed them out. Sooner or later you will be hearing from these credit companies, who will be asking you to pay the now-overdue bills. When you say, "But I don't have an account with your company," they will not believe you, and you may have to expend much time and energy to vindicate yourself.

The other possibility, however, is that the creditors will be unable to locate you, and after some time these bad accounts will then be reported to the credit bureaus, putting a black mark on your credit report. When you receive those credit offers in the mail, if you aren't going to use them, be sure to shred the paperwork right away.

There is a simple way to prevent scam artists from tampering with your mail. Never put your mail in bins or boxes that other people have access to. We used to have such a public drop, a large U.S. Postal bin, on the main floor of the building where I lease my office. Anybody could easily have walked in off the street and taken a handful of mail. Fortunately, the local post office removed the open bin and put a regular mail box on the front entry curb.

In one example of intercepted mail, a murder contract was sent to a person at a business, but a Spanish-speaking employee accidentally intercepted the contract, thinking that this was his mail. Not knowing how to read English, he had a friend read the letter to him. The letter discussed the amount of money that had already been paid for the murder, as well as the daily routine of the target victim, including what parking lot he used every evening when he stopped off at a bar on the way home. There were even such details in the letter as where the hit man was to park and position himself and when a good time would be to kill the target victim!

Obviously, that was a letter that both your local homicide bureau and the U.S. Postal Inspector would want to hear about. But they also want to hear about mail fraud. If fraud is committed against you that involves any use of the mail system to send the fraudulent document, then you should contact your local U.S. Postal Inspector. He will tell you if the fraudulent act falls under the laws involving the Postal Inspection Service.

Be careful what you put in the trash.

You need to know that once you "put out" your trash, including any and all documents, that garbage now belongs to the public. Your right to privacy does not extend to the dumpster, the curb, or wherever it is that your garbage ends up. A few years ago I was working a case for a famous entertainer who, of course, will remain anonymous. He suspected his bookkeeper of some wrongdoing, and I retained the services of a private investigator to do a "garbage run." I discovered that a good investigator can snatch up the entire contents of a ninety-gallon trash barrel in about thirty seconds.

You can learn a lot about a person's personal affairs and business dealings and connections simply by going through his trash. I know, it's a dirty job, but sometimes somebody has to do it. Scam artists also know about this little secret, and now that you know it too, you should consider the nature of your business trash. Do these documents you are throwing away each day contain information about important clients? Do they contain trade secrets, codes, social security numbers, or perhaps your business strategy for the new year?

Everyone should go through this exercise: for a five-day period, every time your hand moves to the wastepaper basket, you should stop and think, "Is this something I want my competitor, the media, an enemy, or a scam artist to have?" If it is of a confidential or personal nature, put it in a box to be shredded later. And by all means, if you haven't bought a good shredder yet, do so now. Make sure that it shreds both vertically and horizontally, as documents shredded vertically only can be restored.

I know this because I have worked cases in which I was asked to restore previously shredded documents. This is not difficult to do, as standard shredding machines shred documents only lengthwise as the document is being fed into the machine. This is better than nothing, but a persistent person could restore such documents. It is much more effective and provides greater protection of proprietary information to use a shredder that uses a two-step process called "cross-cut": that is, it shreds documents not only lengthwise (vertically), but horizontally as well. The resulting fragments are confetti rather than eleven-inch strands of paper.

Checklist: General Office Do's and Don'ts

1. Do secure your office when you go to lunch or a meeting or leave for the day.

2. Do not put your mail in a common bin where passersby may have access to it.

3. Do shred credit card offers instead of just throwing them in the trash can.

4. Do consider what you are throwing in the trash. Shred documents containing any proprietary or sensitive information.

SIX

RECOGNIZING BOGUS
NEGOTIABLE INSTRUMENTS

*Accepting Checks, Money Orders,
Cashier's Checks, and Traveler's Checks*

M ore than 1.4 million checks are forged every day, causing $27.3 million in daily losses to American businesses. According to the National Check Fraud Center, check fraud and counter-feiting are among the fastest-growing problems affecting the nation's financial system, producing estimated annual losses of $10 billion and continuing to rise at an alarming rate annually.

Businesses accepting negotiable instruments such as checks, money orders, or warrants need clerks and cashiers who are able to tell whether these items are genuine or fake. The vast majority of these "sentries of revenue" are in their late teens and early twenties. But even though they are green behind the ears, they can effectively recognize fraud if they are properly trained.

The Anatomy of an Authentic Check

To learn to recognize bogus checks you must first learn to recognize the details found on authentic, legitimate checks. Traditional checks are made using three printing methods:

1. offset lithography (discussed in chapter 1), which produces the majority of the check, including logos, background texture, and personalized information.

2. letter press, which makes the check numbers.

3. magnetically encoded ink, which is used by the letterpress method to imprint the MICR numbers.

I use the word "traditional" above because these have been the methods used in the past to print most personal and business checks. Today there are software programs that can create legitimate checks using a home or office computer and printer. The check stock material comes laser-perforated, three checks to an 8 ½" x 11" sheet of paper, which feeds right into the computer printer like a normal sheet of paper. These checks appear—and are—authentic in their own right, even though they are imprinted with a single printing technology rather than with the traditional three-process method.

The problem is that criminals can use this same technology. When counterfeiters and forgers are trying to pass worthless checks, they want those checks to look as authentic as possible, so they like to use this modern technology. However, they often drop the ball in accurately reproducing the small details of the check. You can learn to recognize a bogus check by examining these details.

Figure 6.1 explains check terminology. There are reasons checks contain the information that they do. When you think about it, there is a person with money (the account holder) who has that money sitting at the local bank (drawee bank). The account holder wants to pay another person money (the payee), so the account holder needs a way to tell his bank to give that person his money. The bank says "OK," but they need certain information. They need to know what amount to pay the payee, and they need to know the date to pay. They need the account holder's signature to authorize the deal, and they also need the account holder's account number.

The personalized information on the check is the personal information about the account holder. I'm sure that your name and your address appear on your checks. Perhaps even your phone number appears if you also requested that it be printed on your checks. However, this is a bad idea—for many reasons. I recommend that you not have your phone number, social security number, or driver's license number printed on your checks.

The date entered is the date upon which the check may be paid.

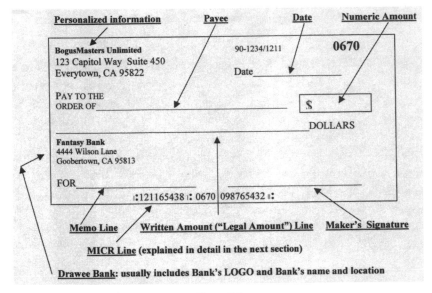

Figure 6.1

Banks do not usually pay checks that are postdated until the date arrives. The payee is the person who is going to receive the amount of money that has been filled out on the check. The numeric amount is the amount of money written numerically, while the written amount line is the amount of the check expressed in handwriting or hand printing (verbiage). The written amount line is also called the "legal amount" line because whenever there is a discrepancy between the amounts showing on the numeric line and the written line, the written amount line is the amount paid.

The maker's signature is the account holder's signature on the front of the check at the lower right side. Bank employees and fraud investigators refer to this as simply "the maker." The memo line is that line to the left of the maker's signature line along the bottom of the check where the account holder may make some optional entry as to the purpose of the check. The drawee bank also must show on the check because that is the institution that has the money to be transferred.

Finally, on the reverse side of the check is a line for the payee to sign or stamp his or her name or company name, which is called the endorsement. This endorsement is the demand to the drawee bank to issue the funds written on the check from the account number shown on the MICR line.

MICR numbers (pronounced "Mike-er") are the "Magnetic Ink Character Recognition" numbers. The toner that prints these numbers contains enough magnetic particles that machines in clearinghouses are able to read and process them automatically. The MICR number on a check is made up of three groups of numbers. The first group is the Bank's ABA (or "SWIFT") number, the second group is the individual check number, and the third group of numbers is the account holder's individual bank account number.

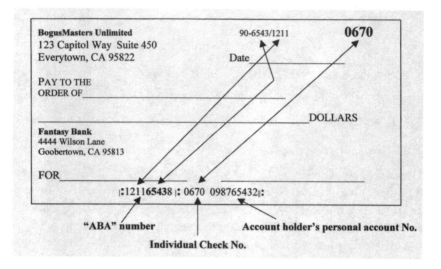

Figure 6.2

Note that the numbers "1211" and "6543" at the beginning of the MICR line are repeated at the top of the check above the date. Also note the repetition of the check number "0670."

Let's begin by dissecting the first group of numbers, the Bank ABA number, where we will find two points of numeric repetition elsewhere on the check. The first two magnetic numbers at the bottom of the check within the brackets |: 12 |: indicate the Federal Reserve District location of the bank on which the check is drawn. The 3rd number, in this case a "1," is the Federal Reserve District Office. The 4th number (also a "1") is the bank's special collection arrangement number or clearinghouse code. Supposedly this is the length of time it takes the check to reach the clearinghouse (1 day, 2 days, or the same day represented by a "0"). These four numbers, along with the following numbers, compose the bank's ABA number.

A repetition of the check number in the MICR line appears at the upper right corner of the check. The remaining numbers represent the account holder's own personal bank account number. These groups of MICR numbers may be arranged in a different order, but even if they are, you should still have the repetition of the numeric information at the top of the check.

Now that you have absorbed this information, we add it to other common information used by merchants to determine whether checks are valid or bogus. What follows is a checklist of things to consider when deciding whether or not you should accept a person's tendered check. I know this might seem like a lot to do when you have a line of customers, but a trained and practiced cashier can cover these details in a few seconds.

Steps for Detecting Fraudulent Checks

1. **Compare the MICR numbers with the top of the check.**
   "Three sets of four digits" should match up. Keep in mind that just because a check may pass this test does not mean that it is a good check. But if the check fails this test, then it should not be accepted.

2. **Confirm the status of the account number on the check.**
   The final group of MICR numbers are the actual customer's account number at the bank. This long number will not repeat on other areas of the legitimate check, but this is a number that can be used to see if there are any negative reports against this account. You should have an arrangement with a vendor who can provide you information as to the status of checks. For example, Costco has a service for its Executive members who, in addition to being able to accept major credit cards, also have the ability to input the account numbers of checks to see if there are any problems with the account.

3. **Accept only pre-printed, personalized checks.**
   The preprinted name and address of the presenter should

agree with this same information on the driver's license or whatever identification card you honor or accept. It is amazing to me what clerks will accept from customers. I've seen personalized information on checks that has been whited out and then re-personalized by hand, with even bank tellers accepting such obviously bogus items!

Remember this motto: "If it looks bogus, it probably is."

4. Consider the presenter's attitude.

Maybe you are not a great judge of character, but I'm sure that you have noticed different attitudes of customers, both good and bad, when they have presented checks. If a person has a bad attitude about providing identification for a check, you probably shouldn't accept that check. Most customers should understand the importance of providing formal identification to accompany a personal check.

Also, watch out for people writing checks who are in a big hurry. Maybe they really are in a hurry, or maybe they are trying to pass a bad check. If a customer is in a hurry and also presents a check with a low check number (see Item 7 below), that's two strikes. I would ask for a second identification at that point.

5. Don't accept starter checks or counter checks.

Explain to your employees the difference between a "starter check," a "counter check," and a "personalized check." A personalized check is one that is pre-printed with the presenter's name and address, whereas starter checks and counter checks are essentially blank checks that have not been personalized. Accept only personalized checks bearing correct information that coincides with the presenter's identification.

6. Look for a perforated side.

Inspect the check to see if it has perforations along at least one side. Legitimate checks are almost always perforated on at least one side, usually along the top or left side.

7. Avoid checks with low check numbers.

Be wary of checks that have low check numbers on them. Anything less than two hundred should at least call for some suspicion. Maybe the customer just moved to town—or maybe he's a forger.

8. **Watch out for pre-written checks.**

   Personal checks should be written in your presence and dated accurately. Checks that are already filled out should cause some suspicion. Have your cashier casually glance over to see if the customer is really filling out the check, or if a portion of it has already been filled out. Savvy forgers know enough to have other people fill out most of a check for them so that if they get caught during a later investigation, little of their own handwriting will be on the check.

9. **Have the customer fill in the payee.**

   Don't use a company rubber stamp as a payee, and don't use other equipment that fills out the check electronically. I know that many larger merchandise businesses are now using this equipment; however, it is important to have the customer fill out the check in its entirety. Later, if you have been the victim of a customer passing worthless checks, the best way to prove the suspect's involvement is to identify his or her handwriting on all of the check. Showing that the suspect prepared the check demonstrates both involvement and intent—so the more handwriting on the check by the presenter, the better.

10. **Verify the presenter's identification (see below).**

    It is quite common for a bad check passer to support the transaction with a bogus identification. Make sure your cashiers and tellers are very familiar with identification documents in your area.

The Inkless Fingerprint System: A Deterrent to Check Fraud

The inkless fingerprint program, which is described in detail in Chapter 11, is a system that allows merchants and bankers to easily obtain a thumbprint from customers when they make a transaction. Many types of businesses, such as food stores, check cashing stores, and most banks and credit unions, have implemented similar programs. The benefits of the program are best exemplified by the following examples. During 1997, a small pizza parlor chain with no thumbprint program suffered losses due to check fraud in the amount of $22,798. In 1998 they instituted the thumbprint program, and their losses due to check fraud decreased by $16,000. Similarly, after implementing the thumbprint program, Raley's food stores saw their losses due to counterfeit two-party checks decrease by 60%.

Guarantee Cards and Warrants

As far as accepting check guarantee cards, your company needs to have an agreement with the authorizing source, or that check guarantee card may be worthless. Avoid accepting two-party checks because you don't have the account holder in front of you to take his or her identification; all you have is the payee. Maybe the payee accepted that check in good faith, but he himself is being duped.

You should also know that much fraud is perpetrated with government assistance warrants. Again, such items can be counterfeited. If you are in a position to accept a volume of these items, it's a good idea to have a local welfare fraud investigator come and give a presentation to your clerks. You might have a training evening or Saturday during which he could come at the same time as a DMV Investigator who talks about valid identifications.

Cashier's Checks, Money Orders, and Traveler's Checks

Since these negotiable items are tendered less frequently than personal checks, your clerks and cashiers have less experience negotiating them. So let's take a look at the peculiarities of each of these negotiable items.

Cashier's Checks

Cashier's checks are issued by individual banks. Banks can either issue them from cash received, or they can deduct the amount of the check, plus a fee, from the customer's account. Cashier's checks are often written for higher dollar amounts than personal checks, sometimes even in the tens of thousands of dollars. If the check looks official enough, your clerks may give away thousands of dollars' worth of product or services to a thief. I call this "grand theft with blind cooperation." Just because a cashier's check was imprinted by a check writer machine (the mechanical printing on the legal amount line) and has other features that make it look valid, does not ensure that the check is authentic. Don't let the official-looking portions of the check fool you into accepting it. Figure 6.3 shows two official-looking counterfeited checks that were accepted.

Figure 6.3

In Figure 6.3 these two checks were accepted because they gave many appearances of authenticity.

The cashier's checks depicted in Figure 6.3 appeared authentic because they exhibited most of the official features of many authentic cashier's checks. The paper stock was a heavier paper with texture to it; the checks had bank logos on them; the written amount line was imprinted by a Paymaster check writing machine, and the remainder of the check was filled out using a typewriter.

These particular negotiable items can wreak a lot of havoc. "Hit and Run" is only one of many fraud schemes using these bogus checks. In this scheme a swindler moves into a town and orders merchandise COD, paying with phony cashier's checks. By the time the counterfeit check bounces, the skip artist has moved on to a new location to repeat the scam. It's probably not a good idea to send out your merchandise COD unless you know the particular company's reputation or you have a business history with the company.

Remember the story I told you in Chapter 1 about the con artist who found people selling diamonds in the classifieds? As you recall, he also used bogus cashier's checks to buy these diamonds. And in still another story, a few years back a nationwide alert went out to jewelers concerning a new twist in counterfeit cashier's check schemes. The suspect would visit the store, select jewelry to be purchased, and obtain the exact price, including tax. The suspect would then leave the store. Upon his return he would offer a cashier's check drawn on an out-of-state bank, together with an identification. The jeweler would then attempt to verify the check.

The jeweler or manager would call information and receive a phone number for a United Fidelity Bank. The phone number was answered by an "operator" who announced, "United Fidelity Bank." When the jeweler indicated that he was calling to verify a cashier's check, the operator said she would switch the call to "customer service." Another voice would then answer "customer service" and follow the standard procedure for check verification.

However, a questioning jeweler, after following the above procedure, was still suspicious and called his local bank. An officer there tried but could not locate the suspect bank in any directory. The bank officer then called "United Fidelity Bank" on a pretext and requested certain information that was needed for a domestic money transfer. The answers he was given convinced him that this "bank" was fictitious.

These stories illustrate the audacity and cunning of some fraud artists. Don't trust everyone who comes in your door, and be sure to go through the steps necessary to verify negotiable instruments. All merchants, car dealerships, businesses—in fact, everyone accepting cashier's checks should exercise extra care when verifying them, particularly when the checks are drawn on an unfamiliar bank. Remember this motto: *Retention is always better than apprehension.* In other words, hanging on to your money or product now by carefully and thoughtfully guarding it is always better than trying to get it back later if you've been scammed. If you have accepted a bogus cashier's check, the chances of recovering your assets are slim. So you should confirm from the beginning that the check is authentic.

Checklist: Authenticating Cashier's Checks

1. Make sure this negotiable instrument was not color copied. If it was, then it is bogus. This subject is discussed further below in "Using a loupe to determine the reproduction process."

2. The use of white-out would be a sign of a bogus cashier's check.

3. Be sure that none of the numbers on the check appear to have been altered.

4. Call your local bank officer to verify the validity of the instrument with the issuing bank. Set up a special arrangement with your bank to provide this service to you, and keep your local bank officer's phone number handy for this purpose.

5. If you have accepted a bogus cashier's check, contact your local law enforcement agency, whether Financial Crimes, Theft, or Property Crimes Bureaus (whichever applies in your area), and submit the check to them for investigation.

Money Orders

Money orders are generally issued by corporations rather than by financial institutions or governments. The obvious exception to this is the money order issued by the U.S. Postal Service, yet the Postal Service is a corporation that just happens to be wholly owned by the U.S. government. The issuing corporation must be prominently noted on the face of the money order. The financial strength of this corporation is important to consider when accepting money orders. If the corporation goes bankrupt or out of business, then the money orders will most likely be worthless.

Major corporations that issue money orders have different format configurations for dollar amount thresholds of the orders. Usually these are noted in color backgrounds, with the dollar amount range for a money order of that color prominently located on the front. Postal money orders do not have the color amount system, but they do use safeguards to prevent the alteration of the dollar amount or payee, as well as other safeguards to deter counterfeiting of the orders themselves. These include color distortion of the design if the original amount is erased, in addition to the use of a security thread and a portrait watermark that becomes visible when held to the light. Since 1989, when the newest version was introduced, postal money orders have been one of the hardest types to alter. Literature on postal money orders is available from the U.S. Postal Inspector's Office in all major cities.

Checklist: Authenticating Money Orders

1. Make sure this negotiable instrument was not color copied. If it was, then it is bogus. This subject is discussed further below in "Using a loupe to determine the reproduction process."

2. Ensure that the money order was not "raised." Read the fine print on money orders; some of them have a dollar-amount limit. Make sure that the amount on the money order is not more than the restricted amount in small print.

3. Look for missing portions of the background, or "bleaching," as an indicator of alteration.

4. Look for the legitimate presence of watermarks, security threads, or other known measures to authenticate legitimate money orders.

Traveler's Checks

In one case involving bogus VISA Bank of America traveler's checks, they had been photocopied on a color laser copy machine. The suspect admitted that he had "found" the checks in Los Angeles, and he also admitted to forging and passing them in San Francisco and Sacramento; however, he claimed that he did not know these were counterfeited traveler's checks. Microscopic examination of the checks revealed several interesting things.

First, each of these checks exhibited laser "pitch" lines that are characteristic of Canon color laser copiers. They also revealed color separation: that is, instead of the genuine offset lithography method used in printing the authentic VISA traveler's checks, in which blue ink is used to create the color blue, these counterfeited checks exhibited fine lines of magenta and cyan in close proximity to one another. When combined with the whiteness of the paper, these lines gave the illusion of blue to the naked eye.

Figure 6.4

Macrophotograph of Visa traveler's check. Even at this enlargement, the image appears to represent an authentic traveler's check.

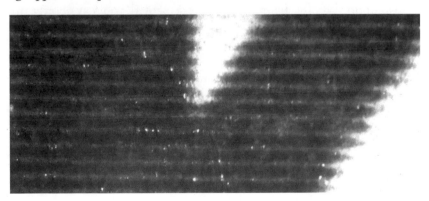

Figure 6.5

Photomicrograph of the lower portion of the "V" in VISA. This photo shows the vertical "pitch" lines. Although this is a black and white image, the heavier lines on the counterfeit check are cyan (blue) while the lighter lines in between are magenta (red).

Figure 6.4, although a black and white image, appears to look authentic. This brings me to a safeguard you can practice to determine the validity of not only traveler's checks, but also money orders and cashier's checks.

Use a loupe to determine the reproduction process.

A loupe is just a small magnifying device. A word of caution, however: if you or your employees are going to use a loupe, then you should be sure of what you are looking for and be able to accurately interpret what you are seeing. I can use a loupe and be able to tell right away what process was used to create a negotiable instrument and whether or not that was the proper process for that particular instrument. Your employees will need training in order to be able to do the same. Properly trained, however, they will be able to use this tool as an invaluable safeguard against fraud.

A loupe will help you to see whether or not a negotiable item or identification has been color copied. Do the colors appear even when viewed through the loupe, or is there color separation indicative of color copiers? In authentic offset lithography processes, the colors are blended, or even in appearance. Color-copied documents exhibit color separations, which may appear as lines with slight separations in magenta, cyan and yellow; or instead of straight lines that are separated, you may observe the color separation in blotches. In either event, if color-copied, the color will be neither consistent nor blended, as it would be in offset lithography and/or intaglio printing.

Intaglio printing is also called "engraved" printing. It characterizes itself by the ink's being raised above the paper, as you can observe and feel on authentic U.S. currency. Engraved printing is almost always a mark of authenticity whenever you observe it on negotiable items. Since this printing method is so expensive, counterfeiters rarely use it.

American Express traveler's checks used to be intaglio printed; however, in recent years they have changed their printing method to offset lithography. But you need to keep in mind that the older American Express traveler's checks are still in circulation, and you may come across some that are intaglio printed. You can consider these as genuine. Just remember this: legitimate American Express traveler's checks will never be color copied. So when you recognize one of these tendered checks as a color copy, do not accept it.

Figure 6.6

Figure 6.6 exhibits a legitimate American Express traveler's check that was created by means of offset-lithography.

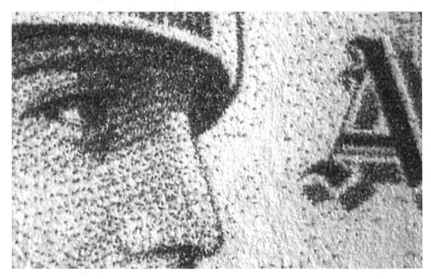

Figure 6.7

Figure 6.7 exhibits a bogus American Express traveler's check that has been color copied.

The new versions of legitimate American Express Travelers Checks ("Cheques") will exhibit these additional security features: There is an offset holographic foil that alternates between the image of the Centurion and the AMERICAN EXPRESS logo when tilted back and forth. This silver hologram also shows the denomination, the amount of which should be repeated elsewhere on the check. When the check is held up to the light, you will also observe an imbedded security thread running vertically in the middle area, as well as a watermark of the Centurion on the rightmost side. As a final test, moisten your finger and rub it across the printed denomination amount, ie. "US $20," on the back of the check just to the left of the blue AMERICAN EXPRESS logo. The ink on this side of the logo will smear, as a water-soluble ink was used to print the left side, but not the right side.

Checklist: Authenticating Traveler's Checks

1. Make sure this negotiable instrument was not color copied. If it was, then it is bogus.

2. Make sure that traveler's checks are countersigned. Also, have the person presenting the check fill in your company name as the payee.

3. Obtain identifying documents, such as a valid driver's license.

"Safe Hours" and Negotiable Instruments

If you run any type of business that accepts checks in exchange for merchandise, foods, or services, then you are most vulnerable to bad checks from Friday evening at 4:00 p.m. through the following Monday morning. Scam artists passing stolen, altered, forged, worthless, or counterfeited negotiable instruments know that the best time to pass these items is over the weekend. That's when the banks are closed and merchants cannot call to verify funds. Many times the checks used don't yet have a bad history and will not turn up any negative remarks when you query their status on the system. In addition, many business owners want to enjoy their weekends, so they leave the business to the novices. So make sure you have properly trained your employees regarding acceptance and rejection of negotiable instruments.

Accepting Identifications

In today's world of color copiers and home computers, it is very easy to create a good-quality bogus identification. Make sure your clerks are familiar with your state's valid identifications. Often you can have a local DMV investigator or fraud investigator give a short presentation to your employees on the hallmarks of authentic identifications. You should review layout, holograms, and other information on the particular ID to make sure it is valid.

Checklist: Authenticating Identifications

1. Look at the date on the driver's license. An expired driver's license is not a valid identification.

2. Do not accept a temporary driver's license.

3. Make sure the age and gender of the person standing in front of you match the information on the ID.

4. Compare the pre-printed address of the maker on the check with the address on the driver's license. If they are different, be cautious and require more backup ID that shows the appropriate address. It's possible that the person has just moved, but it's also possible that he or she is trying to rip you off.

5. Write the driver's license number on the front of the check, as well as the initials of the clerk who accepts it.

RECOGNIZING COUNTERFEIT U.S. CURRENCY

All that Glitters is Not Gold

"To counterfeit" can be defined as "to copy or imitate, without authority or right and with a view to deceive or defraud by passing the thing copied for that which is original or genuine." Although in the past counterfeiters have used offset printing methods, today the tools of counterfeiters are high-tech color copies and computers. The $100 bill is perhaps the favorite denomination of counterfeiters, followed by the $20 bill.

Although the government has greatly improved the quality of printed U.S. currency, in fiscal year 1999, $180 million in counterfeit money was reported. All over the country, businesses have innocently accepted counterfeited U.S. currency, thinking they were getting the "real deal." You need to be aware that the last holder of the note becomes the victim—and that will be you if you inadvertently accept counterfeit currency.

Although counterfeiting is less of a problem now than in the past, it is still something to watch out for, as counterfeit rings have their seasons of striking different areas in the United States. In California we were hit each year off of corridors of our major freeways by "The Highway 101 Counterfeiters." In 1991 counterfeited U.S. currency began to appear in Northern California in cities and towns along highway 101 as well as along the Interstate 80 corridors. Since they are always on the move, counterfeiters often strike larger cities along major interstate highways.

Many counterfeiters use photocopied bills in change or vending machines. If you own a Laundromat, car wash, miniature golf course, or fun park where change machines are used, be on the lookout for bogus U.S. currency in denominations of ones, fives, tens, and twenties that can simply be photocopied from originals, cut to size, and run through your machines. I have actually seen such bills that had been oven-baked to stiffen up the pliable paper they were printed on. In one such case, when local detectives acted on a search warrant, they discovered counterfeited bills with oven rack lines on them!

Although they were fairly crude, these bills were good enough to be accepted by many merchants around town, and they were good enough to clean out change machines. This might sound like an insignificant loss, but if you fall victim to this scheme, you could lose hundreds of dollars in one night. When you lease or buy these change machines, ensure that they are of good enough quality not to accept bogus currency.

In the old days it was the skilled craftsman who manufactured countless scores of counterfeit bills using offset lithographic printing methods. Back then, only a few people were making the majority of the counterfeit bills that entered circulation. Today the tables have turned, and many people are now making smaller quantities of counterfeit money using home scanners, imaging software, ink-jet printers, or color copier machines.

You should train your cashiers to know how to quickly tell the difference between real and fake U.S. currency. They need to know what authentic currency looks and feels like, and they need to take a few seconds to examine each bill carefully. The best way to recognize a counterfeit note is to compare it with a genuine bill of the same denomination and series. Rubbing a bill will not prove whether it is genuine or counterfeit, as ink will rub off either type of note.

Security Features of the New U.S. Currency

In the fall of 1997 the new $100 bills were released by the U.S. Treasury Department, and the lower denominations soon followed. The following is a list of security features of the new U.S. currency, using the $100 denomination as an example. The first four items on this list are the fastest ways to tell if a bill is authentic.

1. The note should not exhibit evidence of being color copied. See Chapter 6 for a more detailed discussion of detecting color-copied items.

Figure 7.1

Figure 7.1 is a macro-photograph of a counterfeited $20 bill made with an ink-jet printer.

Figure 7.2

Figure 7.2 is a photo of authentic U.S. currency. Note the difference in quality as compared to the Figure 7.1 counterfeit.

2. Security threads are imbedded into the fabric. When held to the light, the denomination of the note can be read in the thread. Under ultraviolet light the thread glows a color specific to the denomination (see table below).

3. A watermark of Ben Franklin is on the right side of the front of the bill. Hold the bill up to a light or window to see it.

4. The denomination at the lower right corner on the front of the note is printed in a special ink that shifts color from green to black as you change the viewing angle.

5. There is a larger portrait of Ben Franklin on the new bills, which is offset to the left.

6. The micro-printing of "United States of America" is on Ben's coat (your loupe can come in handy here too; see Chapter 6).

In May 2000 the new $5 and $10 denominations came out. The security features of the $5 and $10 dollar bills are similar to those of the higher denominations.

1. Larger, off-center image of Abraham Lincoln or Alexander Hamilton.

2. Watermark, visible when held up to the light, that matches the image of the presidential portrait on the bill.

3. Embedded polymer security threads that glow blue on the new $5 bill and orange on the new $10 bill when exposed to ultraviolet light. These security threads glow green on $20s, yellow on $50s, and red on $100s.

4. Micro-printing (small printing only visible with a magnifying glass).

Although the security features of the new currency are compelling, we will still have to deal with the older currency for many years. Much U.S. currency is outside of our country, and a lot of it that is still inside the country is stashed in safe boxes or under mattresses. In addition, the older bills will remain in circulation until they wear out. Therefore, here is a table of differences between counterfeit and genuine (older) U.S. currency. As you can see, good quality is the main indicator of authentic U.S. currency.

Counterfeit vs. Genuine U. S. Currency

Counterfeit	Genuine
Portrait	
Portrait is lifeless and the background is usually too dark. Portrait merges into the background. The hairlines are not distinct.	Portrait appears lifelike and stands out distinctly from the fine screen-like background. The hairlines are distinct.
Colored Seal	
Saw-tooth points on the circumference are usually uneven, blunt, or broken off.	Saw-tooth points are even, clear, and sharp.
Border	
The fine lines that crisscross are not clear or distinct.	The fine lines are clear, distinct, and unbroken.
Serial Numbers	
The serial numbers may be in the wrong color. They may not be properly spaced or aligned. Many bills may have the same serial number.	Serial numbers are evenly spaced and aligned. They have a distinctive style. No two genuine bills will have the same serial number.
Watermarks	
No watermarks of president, but may contain some other watermark.	The newer denominations contain a watermark of the president, but the older denominations have no watermarks whatsoever.

Paper

No red and blue fibers embedded in the paper. Red and blue marks may be printed or drawn to resemble fibers.

Red and blue fibers embedded into paper.

Security Thread

No security thread will be present in the newer style bills; however, a printed line may be placed in the proper position, but will not show denomination or glow under UV light.

New style currency will have a thread that when held to the light will reveal the denomination of the bill, and when illuminated by UV light will glow different colors depending on the denomination.

Intaglio Printing

"United States of America" on front of bill will be flat and won't be felt when finger is run lightly across it.

"United States of America" on the front will be raised and can be felt.

Additional Methods for Recognizing Counterfeit Currency

1. Know your dead presidents.

OK, so Benjamin Franklin was not a president. Still, you should check to ensure that the correct portrait appears on the correct denomination. For example, Andrew Jackson should appear on the face of a $20 bill with the design of the White House on the back, and Benjamin Franklin should appear on the face of a $100 bill with a picture of Independence Hall on its reverse side.

Denomination	Portrait on front	Design on back
$1	George Washington	Great Seal of the United States
$5	Abraham Lincoln	Lincoln Memorial

$10	Alexander Hamilton	U.S. Treasury Building
$20	Andrew Jackson	White House
$50	Ulysses S. Grant	U.S. Capitol
$100	Benjamin Franklin	Independence Hall

2. Look for matching numbers (to detect "raised bills").

Look through the green treasury seal on the front of the bill: does the dollar amount shown match the amount on the borders? The other matching numbers test is to turn the bill over and confirm that the numbers on both sides match. One of the tricks of the counterfeiter is to take $1 bills and chemically remove the numbers on the four corners of the front of the bill, leaving the reverse side untouched. Then, using a template from a real $100 bill, he copies the numbers from the $100 denomination onto the corners of the one-dollar bill, creating what is called a "raised instrument." This trick is being successfully performed all over the country; however, your trained employees, by just taking a few extra seconds before putting the money in the till, can catch such fraud before it happens.

Figure 7.3

Just to the right of Ben's portrait you can see the word "ONE" through the treasury seal. This was originally a $1 bill with the four corners "raised" and the portrait of Ben substituted for George.

Figure 7.3 was originally a true $1 bill. By using the method described above, the counterfeiter was able to change the four corners and portrait, but he was not able to completely erase the "ONE" that is over the green treasury seal. To do so would have raised suspicion, since it would have damaged the look of the treasury seal. Instead of "ONE," the number "100" appears through the treasury seal on authentic $100 bills.

3. Use the tactile test (the feel test).

U.S. currency, both old and new, is intaglio printed. An intaglio is an engraving or etched design in hard materials depressed below the surface of the print-face material, so that when printed, an impression from the design yields an image in relief. This three-dimensional, "raised" effect is most difficult to reproduce, and counterfeiters find it much easier—and still effective—to use other reproduction processes, whether ink-jet printers or simple color copying machines.

As a result of the intaglio printing method, certain portions of the ink on authentic U.S. currency sit over the top of the paper, and by lightly running your fingers over the bill, you can tell whether it is flat or textured. If it feels flat, without texture, then it is counterfeit. This is a very simple test, and you should commit a few minutes to practicing this procedure when you take on new employees; then every once in a while, check to make sure that they still "have the touch." Caution: you should test your personal skills for accuracy as to this "feel test" because some people's tactile senses may not be acute enough to tell whether or not a bill is authentic.

4. Use a "PH" pen.

A PH pen is like a highlighting pen, only it does a quick chemical test for you. Applying the pen to U.S. currency will usually turn the note brown, which is an indication that at least the paper stock is correct. The PH pen works the same way on both the old and the new currency. However, do not rely entirely on the PH pen to detect counterfeit currency. The chemical in the pen reacts to the starch in paper, but some types of hair spray can block the starch and the pen chemical from interacting, thus falsely identifying bogus paper as the genuine type. You should still check to make sure that the note itself has not been raised.

PH pens are usually used by bank tellers when they are checking a large series of $100 bills. If you have been hit several times by counterfeit bill scams, you may want to obtain a PH pen for your own use. Be sure to check the instructions on its use and the dates of the U.S. currency to which it applies.

5. Use the loupe to see if the denomination has been color copied (see Chapter 6).

No part of authentic U.S. currency, new or old, was ever made using color copier technology. Therefore, if any of these notes exhibit signs of color copying, they are counterfeit. You can take that to the bank!

When any two of the above procedures cause suspicion and you think you have been presented with a counterfeit bill, first, don't automatically assume that the presenter is the counterfeiter. He might have accepted the counterfeit bill from someone else and is just passing it on in good faith. Having said that, here are the guidelines recommended by the U.S. Secret Service if you suspect a counterfeit note:

1. Do not put yourself in danger.

2. Do not return the bill to the passer.

3. Delay the passer with some excuse, if possible, without risking harm.

4. Telephone the police or the U.S. Secret Service.

5. Observe and record the passer's appearance and that of any companion.

6. Note the license plate number and make of the passer's car.

7. Write your initials and the date on an unprinted portion of the bill, and surrender the note only to the police or a representative from the Secret Service.

You should know that it is a misdemeanor not to surrender counterfeit currency to the U.S. Secret Service (Sec. 492, Title 18, U.S. Code). Besides, the reason the Secret Service wants the money is to get it out of circulation. The counterfeit notes are also an essential part of their investigation since they are used to establish the identity of the passer and the manufacturer.

Now that you have been briefed on bogus negotiable instruments and counterfeit currency, it's time to talk about credit card fraud and how to prevent it.

EIGHT

PREVENTING CREDIT AND DEBIT CARD FRAUD

Extending or Using Credit

C rooks know a good opportunity when they see it. With $40 million being spent on credit sales each day, this field is too fertile to ignore. Con artists will continue to come up with new ways to obtain credit account information in order to rack up charges against unsuspecting account holders. Visa has reported that the losses due to credit card fraud in 1999 amounted to $336 million!

There are several different types of credit card fraud. I will discuss the use of credit and debit cards from the perspective of both the business person or clerk who accepts them and the consumer who uses them. Fraud prevention measures need to be taken on both sides of all transactions.

Counterfeit Credit Cards

Though counterfeit credit cards are often used by small-time operators, they are also the weapon of choice of many organized crime groups. Many of these organizations use the profits gained from counterfeit cards to finance other illegal businesses, such as drug smuggling.

A counterfeit credit card is a white or gray plastic card called "white plastic." Once a magnetic strip is added on the back, the card is ready to use. The white plastics may be silk screened with various bank logos, including the Visa and MasterCard logos. The account number and desired name are embossed on the face of the card using a "Farrington" machine. Stolen information from unsuspecting account holders is encoded on the magnetic strip on the back. White plastics are often made in China, Macau, and Hong Kong, and in their simplest form are most commonly used at gas stations.

The counterfeiters do not need to use actual people's names on their counterfeit cards because they can simply emboss any name to match their bogus identification. With a stolen credit card, the thief has a short time frame in which to operate before the card holder misses the card. The counterfeit card has a longer service life. Since the account number is the only thing stolen and the credit card itself is returned to the customer, the fraud is not detected until the customer reads over the next billing statement. In some cases a fraudulent user has even mailed stolen or counterfeited checks to the bank for payment, thus extending the credit life of the card.

The account numbers for these counterfeit cards are stolen from various types of businesses, such as car rental agencies, hotels, gas stations, and restaurants and taverns—usually by the employees. Counterfeiters pay these employees for each account number and expiration date they obtain. Many employees use "skimmers" to collect good account numbers from customers. A skimmer is a hand-held device that can fit in a person's pocket. It is used to electronically copy the information from a credit card or ATM card to be later sold and used on the black market. Since the use of skimmers is common among restaurant servers, I discuss this use in more detail in Chapter 9.

Counterfeiting organizations call databases and use merchant business codes to ensure that the account numbers are good and a healthy balance is available before they emboss the cards. Counterfeiters can and do buy the encoding and embossing machines on the open market. The encoding can also be done by using a laptop computer in the seat of a car. The clandestine organizations will go to great lengths to conceal this equipment. They will usually have a safe house to which only a few trusted people have access.

It is difficult to track suppliers and users of counterfeit credit cards. Some suppliers organize buyers who travel around the country, buying such expensive items as Rolex watches, jewelry, cosmetics, computers, and photography equipment. With this in mind, the merchant should exercise caution in accepting credit cards for smaller retail items of high dollar value.

Stolen Credit Cards

In addition to stealing and using credit card account numbers, scammers often steal and use the cards themselves. This is the crudest, most straightforward method of credit card fraud. When a credit card is actually stolen, the customer soon realizes that it is missing and reports the card as lost or stolen. In this situation, the thief is quite limited in the amount of fraud he can commit because he has little time to work the card. He may buy gas for his car or make some mail-order purchases, but he could end up leaving a trail to himself if he isn't careful.

To help prevent your employees from accepting any recently stolen credit cards, make sure they know how to get appropriate identification from a customer and how to verify that the card presenter is the true account holder. Just because a card will authorize on the system, that doesn't mean that the person passing it is the true account holder or has permission to use that card. Review with your employees the procedures discussed in Chapter 6 for accepting and verifying identifications.

If your own credit card has been lost or stolen, you need to report it as "lost or stolen." Don't simply close the account. Tell your credit card company to generate a new account number and to overnight-mail new cards to you if you are in a hurry.

Signatures on Credit Cards

The signature card panel on the back of a credit or debit card was placed there as a security device by the card issuer, such as Visa, Mastercard, Discover, or American Express. Each of these card issuers requires that the card holder sign the card before it can be considered valid. This is part of the policy set forth by the card companies, and each merchant who agrees to accept any of these cards agrees in the signed contract to operate within the policy. Cards not bearing a signature, including those with the printed words "See ID," are not within policy. Accepting such cards leaves the merchant vulnerable to "charge-backs" by the company should the card prove to be invalid or stolen.

At a local university, a thief picked the locks of the lockers in the men's gymnasium. He then carefully removed credit cards, replaced the wallets, and re-locked the lockers. The cards were then used to purchase expensive electronic devices, mostly big screen TV's, stereo equipment, and laptop computers, which sell easily on the street. Investigators from the university police, city police, and county sheriff's departments discovered the identity of the thief and arrested him at his home. A search recovered several of the stolen credit cards, of which three were found to have the "See ID" notation on the signature panel. The credit card company investigators obtained copies of the police reports. The companies then charged back the purchases on these three cards, costing the merchants several thousand dollars each.

Falsified Credit Applications

Some crooks obtain legitimate credit cards by stealing and filling out credit applications that were on their way to potential customers. These applications are usually either intercepted in the mail before arriving to the addressee, or retrieved from the addressee's garbage can. Persons posing as spouses, such as ex-girlfriends or roommates, can also obtain cards under such false pretenses.

When the crook fills out the application, he indicates an address change so that the new card is delivered to him. When the card arrives, he then runs up charges until the credit limit is maxed out. When nobody pays the monthly payment, the credit company makes a bad report to the credit-reporting agencies against the original addressee. See Chapter 13 for more information on preventing such an "identity theft" fraud from happening to you.

Checking Account "Debit" Cards (or ATM Cards)

This type of card is tied to your checking account and has a MasterCard or Visa logo on it. However, MasterCard and Visa are just providers of financial transactions for this type of card; they are not extending any credit since the money for the purchases comes out of your checking account.

Debit cards have become very popular with consumers. According to CardTrak Online, debit card use has increased by 40% in dollar volume and 25% in transaction volume over the last couple of years. Consumers are beginning to prefer debit cards over credit cards since the major credit card companies use high late fees and interest rates and other charges that don't exist when using debit cards. During the 1999 holiday season, consumers used debit cards about 500 million times, debiting their checking or savings account for an average of $37.68 per transaction, according to CardWeb's CardData service. Whereas in 1998 there were approximately 99.4 million debit cards in use, it was projected that in 1999 there would be 120 million in use, with $3.1 billion in transactions projected for 1999. These figures will increase through 2001.

As the use of debit cards grows, so too does the fraudulent use of them. Stolen debit cards can be used by thieves anywhere, just like regular credit cards, to make purchases. Your personal identification number (PIN) is not needed unless they would request "cash back," which they won't. One place these crooks like to test the cards to see if they have been reported stolen is at gas stations without surveillance cameras. If they find that the card is still good, they go on a spending spree.

Although debit card transactions are withdrawn from your checking account, in some ways they are more vulnerable to fraud than a check would be. When you write a check, at least you can put a stop payment on the check if you suspect fraud against the account. These debit cards are also subject to the same types of fraud as regular credit cards, with much of this fraud occurring on the Internet. Even President Clinton urged consumers in 1999 not to use debit or check cards over the Internet because protection cannot be guaranteed. You don't know the reputation of the people at the other end taking your card information via "secured servers."

If you use a debit card, there are precautions you can take to help prevent its fraudulent use. One is to keep careful track of your transactions and compare them with your bank statements. There was an elderly man who was in the hospital for some time and was not able to check over his monthly bank statement, which indicated some fraudulent activity on his account. He returned home to discover that all of the money in his checking account had been cleared out, approximately $50,000. This money was part of this man's retirement. When he contacted his bank, he was informed that since he had not reported the fraudulent activity on his account earlier, they were not responsible for this loss and would not cover it.

This points out two things. First, it is important to go over your bank statement carefully every month. If there is a charge that you cannot identify, even a small one of say $5.00, then you need to contact your bank to get an answer as to what it is. The bank may use your failure to report a small fraudulent charge as a reason to justify not returning larger sums of money due to later fraud, making the argument that you should have reported the earlier fraud so that they could have been more vigilant against future fraud occurrences.

Second, this story points out the importance of carefully guarding your debit card and your statement information. You should keep your monthly statements locked up in a safe place, and always be vigilant when using your debit card in public, the same as you would be with your credit card. Also, it would be best to not use your debit card for Internet purchases. If you must use a card to make Internet purchases, do not use your checking account debit card, since the possibility exists that your checking account could be cleared out. Instead, use a regular credit card, exclusively for Internet purchases, that has a low limit of $300, so as to limit the amount of potential fraud against you.

Likely Fraud Sources

Most credit card fraud is perpetrated by someone known by the victim, possibly a family member, employee, or friend. Protect your account number in your own business and in your home. Don't leave cards or statements lying around as a temptation. If you issue credit cards to employees, have them sign an agreement that upon termination of employment, they will return all cards and be liable for all unauthorized charges. Remember to get all company credit cards back when an employee leaves your company.

Extending Credit to Customers

VISA, MasterCard, American Express, and Discover are not the only companies issuing credit cards. Many retailers, such as Macy's, Sears, JC Penney, and Costco, offer credit cards backed by their own respective organizations. Local lumberyards, hardware stores, and many other thousands of businesses around the country extend credit to their customers as well. Perhaps your business has begun offering its own credit cards or credit accounts to your customers. When extending credit to individuals, shortcuts should not be taken in the application process. You must ensure that the people applying for the credit accounts are really who they say they are.

A customer may look clean-cut and spin a good web of confidence, but this respectable-appearing con artist may be using someone else's good name and financial reputation to establish credit with your company. As Shakespeare cautioned in *Macbeth*, "A man may smile and smile, and be a villain." If you think that the applicant for a credit account may not really be who he says he is, you can take additional steps to confirm his identity. You can request additional forms of identification, such as a social security card, driver's license, last pay stub, canceled check, or a utility statement.

Vulnerable Seasons

During the Thanksgiving through Christmas holiday season, most people want to take some time off. This includes not only the owner or manager of a business, but also the veteran clerks and the people paying invoices. This is also a time when people are thinking more about personal affairs than about the details of doing their jobs. As anyone in law enforcement can tell you, this is also the period of greatest fraud involving stolen or forged checks and credit cards, as well as counterfeit instruments.

Therefore, prior to the Thanksgiving holiday, owners and managers should rehearse company policies and procedures regarding accounting practices and cash register practices with seasonal or less experienced help. Review the scams that can be perpetrated against your company, and explain what the employees can do to be vigilant. Any extra help you take on during the holidays will need to be monitored regularly until precautionary procedures become habitual to them.

Checklists: Credit Card Fraud Prevention Measures

When ACCEPTING credit cards:

1. Confirm that the name of the presenter matches the name on the credit card.

2. Confirm that the gender of the presenter matches the gender of the name on the card.

3. Is the card signed on the back? If not, ask for a driver's license to compare with the tendered credit card.

Examine the card's security features:

4. The numbers and letters on the card should be clear and evenly spaced.

5. Holograms should be crisp and not appear contrived.

6. Check the tamper-resistant signature panel. Many of these today have an under-print of the word "Void" so that if a thief tries to erase the true signature from the white signature panel, the white overlay will also be removed, revealing the word "Void" underneath.

7. Check that the number imprint on the reverse side of the card (which will appear backwards, of course) corresponds to the numbers on the face of the card.

8. Check with the organization that provides your merchant services to obtain any specific advice and safeguards for accepting credit cards.

When PROCESSING credit cards and managing information:

1. Do not leave credit card receipts lying around where employees or other customers can get a good look at them.

2. When preparing an invoice or receipt for the customer after a mail-order credit card purchase, don't put the entire credit card number on the invoice; put only the first four or the last four digits. That way the account holder will know which card was used for that purchase, but there won't be any chance of abuse should the customer's mail be intercepted.

3. Make sure computer files containing lists of customer credit card information are not accessible by employees who are not involved in bookkeeping duties.

4. When disposing of old sales invoices and credit card records, use a shredder. If you do a large volume and don't have the time to shred them, put them in a cardboard box, seal it with tape, and call a shredding service, who will come to your location with a truck and shred the entire box and contents.

When USING credit/debit cards:

1. When establishing passwords and personal identification

numbers (PINs), use obscure combinations of numbers and letters. Do not use any obvious information such as the last four digits of your social security number, your birth date, portions of your phone numbers, or the numeric part of your address.

2. Review your bank account statement immediately upon receiving it to ensure that there are no unexplained charges against your account. If there is a charge that you do not understand, contact your bank.

3. Guard your monthly statement information by keeping it locked up in a safe place.

4. When paying by debit card, always ask to swipe the card yourself if possible.

5. Do not lay your credit card on tables or counters while waiting to use your card, as someone may be watching, or even zooming in with a video camera to capture customers' account numbers and expiration dates.

6. Do not use your debit card over the Internet. Use a credit card that has a low limit just for this purpose.

RESTAURANT AND TAVERN PILFERING SCAMS

Don't Let Employees Eat Up Your Profits

T he restaurant and tavern industry as a whole contains the highest number of employees of any industry in the country. Servers and bartenders are usually in their teens and 20s, in high school or college, and they move around and change jobs often. Nevertheless, these young people are creative and learn fast from their more seasoned colleagues. Whether you own a Mom and Pop country pancake house or a nationwide franchise chain, keep your eyes open—if there is a scam to be played out in a restaurant, it can and will be done.

Food Service Scams

Duplicate Check (receipt) Scam

If you offer a buffet in your eatery, beware of the duplicate check scam. Servers know that two people each having a buffet and a soft drink will always cost the same, say $12.50 per person. Since there is no need to ring in any items to retrieve them from the kitchen, the server simply prints a duplicate check from table number 1 and gives it to table number 2. The register thinks that only one table paid when in fact, two paid. The payment for one table goes to the till, but payment for the second table goes into the server's pocket. When the restaurant is busy, the owner or manager will never notice two tables of two parties paying for the same check, but the server gets the $25 from the two people paying at table number 2 plus the tip!

A savvy server will only do this a couple of times a day. It is really difficult to detect this scam because it's hard to nail down how much food people are eating at the buffet. A $25 loss might not seem like much to you, but if all the servers know about this trick (and they do), and you have five servers working each day and each does it once, that's $125 a day. If you are open 325 days in that year, you will lose $40,625!

There are several ways to stop this scam. If you use a video surveillance system, connect the electronic cash register to the video system to capture every transaction, not only visually but also digitally. If you have a computer system that prints receipts, have it keep track of how many reprinted checks it prints. However, an employee may say that he or she had two customers who wanted separate receipts, so you have to be careful not to confront someone who is printing duplicate checks.

If you suspect someone of a duplicate receipt scam, go into the computer and check the time the check was rung in for that particular table. If the time on the computer shows 12:30 p.m., and the server just now gave a check to that table at 3:30 p.m., you have something to work with. You could also have the hostess keep track of how many people she has seated in a particular server's section and compare the numbers.

If you use a numbered check system, don't just give the servers a certain number of checks each day for which they're responsible, because they can just pass off one of them as a duplicate check. What you need to do is give the hostess a certain number of checks at the beginning of the day that are all numbered and logged into a book. She should set one down on the table when she seats the customers. The check needs to display the server's name, table number, and the time at the top. This way, all the checks are accounted for, and each table has to have its own check. Another method to this system is for the hostess to have a sheet at her station containing all the check numbers, and when she places a check on a table, she then writes the server's name in that slot. This way, if a check is missing, you know who has it.

Coupon Scams

If your restaurant occasionally offers coupons in the phone book or in newspaper flyers, BEWARE! If your servers and bartenders keep their own banks and make change for the customers, your coupons could be doing more than just trying to get people in the doors—they could be losing your business a lot of money. Let's suppose a table of customers comes in to dine but doesn't know about the coupon that is available. All the server has to do is get hold of lots of coupons (which is easy), but charge the unsuspecting customers the full price for their purchases. If the table pays in cash, then the server just goes back to the computer, deducts the amount of the coupon, and settles the bill at the reduced amount and pockets the difference.

The server just got tipped on the higher amount, got the dollar value of the coupon in cash, got the excess tax money from the higher bill (that you pay for), and didn't have to pay tax on the extra income. You, as an owner, are completely unaware of the situation because for all you know, the customers just came in off the street with a coupon and used it to pay their bill. This scam is hard to counter. One thing you can do to prevent it is to make the server staple the check and the coupon together. A good video system will also help. If you use video, put a small monitor by the work area to remind employees that they are being filmed.

Discount Scams

Some restaurants offer discounts to senior citizens, 2-for-1 specials on certain days, free meals for kids, town employee discounts, and the infamous frequent-customer card that is stamped or hole punched with a special stamp or hole puncher that EVERY employee has access to. As with the coupons, if an employee is keeping his or her own bank, all he or she has to do, if the customer pays in cash, is to deduct whatever the special is for the day and keep the difference.

How are you, the owner or manager, going to know whether two senior citizens or two college students came in and ate? The check says senior citizen discount, but you may not look at the checks until the next day. Similarly, if people who don't frequent your establishment come in for dinner and they don't know that Tuesday is 2-for-1 night, these out-of-town customers may pay the bill in full while your server makes $13.95 on that second roast beef dinner.

This scam is extremely hard to catch when savvy servers use it sparingly and when your business is offering the discounts, but not keeping track of who is using them. If you can afford not to offer discounts, then don't! But if you must, be sure to make frequent personal visits on busy nights so the employees are aware that you are watching them carefully. If you use frequent customer cards, keep only one stamp or hole punch, and have your manager regulate its use. Another way to control these cards is to have the hostess distribute them only to customers who ask for them. That way you won't have your employees taking the cards, punching holes in them, then giving the cards to their friends for free meals.

Gift Certificate Scams

If your gift certificates are kept at the hostess stand or behind the bar and you allow any employee to sell one, you are in for a big surprise. This will be especially true if the certificates are not numbered or if you use an authorized signature stamp on them instead of signing each one personally. All an employee would have to do is take some gift certificates and stamp them with the owner's signature stamp, then redeem them as cash for one of the customer checks that was already paid with cash. This scammer has just made off with $50 or $100 in cash from your profits. Fortunately, this fraud is a lot easier to minimize if you do the following:

1. Treat gift certificates like cash. Keep them under lock and key, and when one is purchased, have a trusted manager get it—or get it yourself.

2. Always number gift certificates, and have a log of the numbers. Write down who bought each one, who it is for, the date it was sold, and the amount it was sold for.

3. Insist that employees have the customer sign and date the certificate upon redemption.

4. Individually sign each and every gift certificate upon its sale, not beforehand. Never use an authorized rubber stamp to validate its authenticity because it would be easy to copy or duplicate your gift certificate.

5. Remember, gift certificates can be and are counterfeited. Make your certificates individual enough so that you can authenticate each one, and do so at the point of sale, not the next day.

Pilfered Food

If you think that your high food costs are due solely to a few butter pats and creamers ending up in the trash, you are sorely mistaken!

Remember, you have college students working for you who have little money. If they are making off with a bottle of ketchup here, a few hot chocolate packets there, a piece of cake for later—then before you know it, you'll be jacking up your meal prices just to make a profit. You can cut down on employees' food pilfering by locking up refrigerators and coolers after food service hours are over. Also, try to have the changing room or bathrooms away from the supplies area so that the employees won't be loading up their backpacks with your supplies.

Bartender Scams

You can't even imagine how much profit is lost from scams operating behind the bar! It is very difficult to keep track of the amount of beer and liquor that is poured, the quantity provided in each drink, and the amount wasted at the tap. Furthermore, bartenders having full custody of all transactions creates a fertile breeding ground for pilfering scams.

The Memory Scam

If a bartender has worked at your bar for even two weeks, I guarantee that he knows the cost of every drink including tax. Someone comes in for a beer on tap, and the bartender says, "That will be $3.75." The customer pays (usually in cash), change is returned, and nothing is ever rung in. If you have a computer system, the bartender can ring in a large order, see the total, collect the cash, and then delete the order from the computer's memory. All that cash goes to the bartender, and you are none the wiser. Wily bartenders will do this only on non-countable items, such as tapped beer and mixed drinks. They know that you keep inventory of the bottled beer!

You have to be sly to catch an experienced bartender working these scams. Most of the time, the bartenders close the restaurant after the owners and managers go home. This provides free rein for the bartender to cover his trail from the evening's festivities. Here are some suggestions to reduce bartender pilfering:

1. Always keep a manager in your restaurant or tavern until closing.

2. If you have a computer system, occasionally go into the bartender's employee number when there are customers seated at the bar and check what has been rung in.

3. Have an inconspicuous friend come in and watch your bartender to see if he or she is ringing in items as orders are received.

4. Don't let your bartender give any drinks to servers without a purchase slip. For example, a server is busy and runs by the bartender asking for three beers, and the bartender pours them. You may never get them rung in because the server is giving free drinks to friends in the dining room!

5. Make your bartenders give every customer a receipt for what is ordered. If a customer has a tab going, then make the bartender place a receipt in front of the customer that is replaced with every addition to the tab. Although this may cost you a little more in printer paper, your gross sales will increase ten-fold.

Open Drawer/Busy Night Scam

When your restaurant is very busy, the scams get even easier to pull off. A good bartender will take several orders from several people at once. He will know the costs of all the drinks and will add them appropriately, rounding up to the nearest quarter. If the customers are drunk, they won't notice as long as the totals are close to accurate. The bartender mixes the drinks, then collects $4.50 from customer #1, $7.25 from customer #2, and $12.50 from customer #3.

Finally, the bartender goes to the register and rings in only two bottled beers, totaling the $7.25 reported for customer #2, and puts all the money in the drawer. When he balances the till at closing time, he just pockets all the excess cash. The customers never know the difference, and a spy would simply think that the bartender rang in the orders and put the money in the drawer. And you, the owner or manager, would be none the wiser because it happened so quickly and you were busy.

If you have a computer system that requires something to be rung in to open the till, a similar scam would be for the bartender to prop the drawer open with a rag or something else. This way he can get in and out of it without the computer knowing the actual cash amounts coming and going.

Substitution of Liquors

Liquors, as you probably know, come in a range of qualities. The lowest quality of liquor served is called well liquor, with call liquor being a superior grade. Of course, the lower quality liquors are less expensive than the call liquors. A bartender can substitute call liquor with well liquor and then charge the customer for the call liquor. Then the bartender rings up the transaction as a well sale and keeps the difference. This trick is easier to pull off as the night progresses because customers' senses get duller the more they drink. They don't notice that the higher-quality alcohol they are requesting is being substituted with the well liquor.

Short drink Scam

The bartender may underpour four drinks by a quarter of an ounce, then sell that extra ounce as a shot and keep the cash.

Checklist: Minimizing Bartender Scams

1. Be sure you can trust your bartenders! Get a lot of references before hiring them.

2. If you ever see a propped drawer, demand that it be shut at all times. Give the reason that it would be easy for a customer to get into the till from over the counter when the bartender is busy.

3. Know how much alcohol is sold on average on busy nights. That way, when different bartenders have similar volume, but one of them always has low sales revenue, you have good cause to believe that the employee with lower sales is pilfering.

4. Keep a very close inventory of countable items, including a count of bottles of liquor. If you are running through large amounts of liquor but have only a lot of bottled beer rung in, then a BIG RED FLASHING LIGHT should be going off.

5. Beware of free drinks given to local customers and friends— it happens ALL the time.

6. The best system to have is a counted pour system. The bartender has to ring in the drink to activate the pourer, and it pours a $^1/_4$, $^1/_2$, or full ounce depending on the drink. This also helps control the stiff or heavy pourer. Having a heavy-pouring bartender is like pouring money down the drain. Customers like stiff drinks because they think they are getting their money's worth, but that also means you are losing profits and they are ordering fewer drinks. Bartenders know that stiff drinks put more tip money in their pockets, so they serve them!

7. Have the manager balance the bartender's drawer unannounced on occasion at the end of the night. This way, the bartender won't be able to pilfer the extra cash he raked in, plus you will know that he was preparing to skim if the till shows a cash overage.

The pilfering scams I have explained in this section do not cover all the many restaurant and tavern scams that are committed all over the country. Each place has its unique loopholes and security breaches that any employee can figure out with a little time. But my suggestions will make you a wiser business owner by making you aware of what is possible, so that you can reduce scamming and learn how to make your business more profitable.

TEN

MEDICAL MALPRACTICE EXPOSED IN PATIENT CHARTS

Investigative Methods to Reveal Cover-Ups

Keeping Careful Medical Records

Some medical frauds and malpractice cases seem to have it all: life-and death issues of mystery, intrigue, cunning, and deceit. Medical records are so complex that when they come into question, they are often subjected to most or all of the document examinations described in detail in Chapter 2. More commonly than you might think, doctors, nurses, and other medical staff tamper with medical charts and records. To honest and law-abiding people, this revelation must be an abomination. Of course, the great majority of medical professionals are hardworking and honest. They do everything they can to help their patients, including attempting to keep careful and accurate records. Yet there are those unscrupulous folks in the medical profession who, realizing they have made a mistake, use paper, pen, whiteout, and machines to cover their tracks. These types of cases provide a wealth of opportunity for a skilled forensic document expert to uncover the inconsistencies that such tampering creates.

If you are in the medical profession, you and your staff need to avoid the appearance of evil in your medical record keeping because if any dispute arises, and if you happen to have suspicious entries on the medical chart, then you will have a lot of explaining to do. It is far better, of course, to keep complete and accurate records that include pertinent, properly-made entries. That way, if one of your medical files experiences a groundless attack, your perfect record keeping will be your vindication. This leads me to my next point:

You don't have to do anything wrong to be sued. Even if your medical records are flawless, you can still fall victim to a baseless attack in which a patient will make all kinds of groundless allegations. He or she may claim that the medical record has been altered, when in fact, the record is accurate and exhibits no signs of tampering. In such situations, all of the usual questioned document examinations would still need to be conducted in order to establish that nothing is wrong with the medical charts.

I just finished working on a case in which an RN alleged that someone had altered the values of blood pressure and pulse readings that he had made on a chart. I was able to report that microscopic examination had revealed no paper fiber disturbances around the areas of alleged alterations and that infrared examination revealed normal procedure in the use of the writing instrument. In fact, there were no indications at all that any portion of these records had been altered.

In the following paragraphs, I will discuss some of the different aspects of medical records that I explore when I am looking for consistencies and inconsistencies in the overall patient chart. After reading this section, I think you will see why medical records should be kept in strict compliance with industry standards. Sloppy medical records will reflect on other aspects of a patient's care and on the competence of the doctor, nurses, and other medical staff. Standard record-keeping procedures should be reviewed with staff periodically so that everyone contributing to the records will continue to follow correct and consistent practices.

Overall File Consistency

A lot of information goes into a medical file or patient record. In addition to notations about the patient's appearance, the patient's descriptions of symptoms, the doctor's examination notes, and the resulting comments and recommendations, there are other handwritten entries as well, such as raw billing records and prescription records. This additional information should conform to the main handwritten chart entries made over time. All information should be inter-compared from a chronological standpoint to ensure consistency or to reveal fraud.

Here are some questions to consider: Do the diagnostic code entries on the invoice pages agree with the doctor's entries on the chart pages?

That is, if there is an entry on a chart page that reflects a supposed visit by a patient, shouldn't there also be a billing record for that visit? Does the files record of prescribed medications reflect the alleged visit? Was a prescription note truly written there at the alleged time, or was it actually a corrected entry made much later to cover up a mistake? Do the diagnostic records filled out by the doctor in the patient's chart reveal different pens being used? That in itself could be evidence of tampering.

Signatures, Initials, and Handwriting

The handwriting, initials, and signatures on a medical chart are very important in examinations, particularly when an RN or doctor is alleging that a questioned entry was not made by him or her. These examinations attempt to identify who wrote what portions of questioned entries and to eliminate the suspects who were not involved in various questioned writings. Usually, known writings by the various doctors and nurses appear elsewhere on the non-disputed portions of the same medical record; therefore, it is important to obtain copies of the entire medical file when requesting copies via subpoena. I would request color copies of the record because they give a good initial idea of what writing instruments were used.

Infrared Examinations

Infrared examinations can prove that a medical record has been altered. For example, infrared examination of the inks can determine if a different writing instrument was later used to alter an original entry, such as blood pressure or prescribed medications.

Figure 10.1

Figure 10.2

In Figure 10.1, the blood pressure reading appears to be 120/80 when viewed by the naked eye. Even though two different pens were used, the entire entry is in black ink. However, in Figure 10.2, infrared examination reveals that the original entry was really 170/90. The black ink of the second pen glows white, showing where the original entry was altered. This phenomenon is called infrared luminescence. A blue-green light is used to illuminate the questioned entry, while a series of infrared barrier filters are used in front of a CCD digital camera that is connected to a computer and monitor. This procedure can provide proof that a different writing instrument was used to change an original entry.

Conversely, infrared examinations may also demonstrate the lack of differences in writing implements, which can be an important indicator of fraud when a medical chart is involved. One would expect to find a variety of different inks being used in an authentic medical chart, as different entries are recorded at different times by different nurses and doctors. An entire medical chart containing only one type of ink could very well be a re-creation of an original chart that has been destroyed. This has been the case in many medical charts that I have examined.

Another use of infrared technology sometimes allows us to view through the blackness of an obliteration to see what was originally written underneath. When a heavy black pen or marker is used to conceal an entry, it can be made visible again through infrared techniques. When this technique successfully visualizes the obliterated entry, a permanent record can be made as an exhibit to be used in court.

Latent Handwriting Examinations

Latent handwriting examinations of file documents in sequence can reveal the arrangement of chart record pages. This can be used to determine the order the pages were in when the alleged entries were made, revealing whether any pages have later been inserted into the file or if other pages have been removed. This test can also prove details concerning chronology.

Latent writing examinations can also reveal the text from any missing or removed pages, since this text shows itself as impressions on the existing pages in the file. Furthermore, latent writing examinations may reveal that there was backing behind all pages in the record as they were being written, with the exception of the disputed page.

Latent writing tests can also show whether the writer's practice of making medical chart entries was consistent between the questioned and known documents. For example, did the doctor as a matter of course write on chart pages that rested directly on top of older pages behind them, or instead, did the doctor use a backing sheet (usually hard stock) behind the page being written on? The use of a backing sheet would protect the older pages from receiving any latent impressions from the writings on the new sheets added above them. Whichever method you use, maintain consistency in that method so as to avoid confusion should the medical file be processed for latent handwriting impressions in the future.

Examination of Mechanical Impressions

The term *mechanical impressions* usually refers to a device that typed any information on the medical records. Of course, we have to be clear that any text that we think was typewritten may really have been imprinted on the document by a computer printer, whether daisy wheel, dot matrix, laser printer, ink-jet, or some thermal process.

The goal in these examinations is fourfold. First, can we identify which of the various processes were used to type the entry? Second, is there sufficient evidence to actually identify the very machine that typed the entry? Third, can we identify the computer connected to the machine that typed the entry? Fourth, can we establish when the computer and/or printer made said questioned entries on the medical chart?

Examinations of Trace Evidence

There are other obscure areas of significance that most people do not consider, but which can provide answers to the history and keeping of the medical record. These more obscure areas include paper folds, creases, staple/punch holes, paper cutting bar marks, and the use of tape. Further examinations of photocopy processes, rubber stamp impressions, and preprinted forms, as described in Chapter 2, should also be conducted. Another good procedure to follow is to be consistent in your usage of forms. It is best to obtain offset-produced forms to use in your practice, as these are difficult to counterfeit.

Sign-In Sheets

In addition to the medical chart itself, patient sign-in sheets and other such forms can prove critical in some investigations. All medical practitioners should ensure that the patients themselves write their own names on sign-in sheets. If there are other forms that should be filled out only by the patients, be diligent about making sure that only patients themselves fill out these forms. Doctors should also preserve these original records in a safe place. This will be quite important in situations, for example, in which a patient alleges that he or she did not come in for a certain appointment, or was so upset with the doctor that he or she stopped going in for treatments. If you have a sign-in sheet bearing the name handwritten by the patient, that alone will prove the patient's attendance at your office on certain dates.

A case in point: A young woman alleged that a chiropractor had fondled her when he was giving her a massage therapy. In her unwavering deposition testimony, she claimed that she was so upset that she could not and did not return to the office for any further treatments. However, her signature appeared on a clinic registration form on the following day, proving that she did, in fact, return to the office soon after the alleged incident. The signature on that date became disputed, but the chiropractor was able to produce her undisputed signature on numerous other sign-in registers from the previous weeks. These known samples were instrumental in demonstrating that the signature of the day in question was truly made by the young woman. This of course diminished the credibility of her testimony as to her trauma in the alleged fondling incident.

Fraud by Medical Patients

One type of fraud in the medical field occurs when uninsured people pose as medically covered individuals when going to your clinic or the Emergency Room for medical care. They obtain such care by signing an Emergency Consent form in the name of a person who does have coverage. This demonstrates why it is important to verify a patient's identity when he or she comes in for medical consultation or treatment. Your staff should request standard identification documents, such as a driver's license or other document providing a photo identification.

In a different type of patient fraud, an employee forged a doctor's name to a Certification Of Physician pertaining to the Family and Medical Leave Act, and this employee then tendered these falsified forms to his employer to excuse his unauthorized leave. If there is any question about such documents, supervisors should contact the clinic to verify that the doctor or nurse actually filled out the form tendered by the employee. Otherwise they should request that such forms be mailed directly from the clinic to the business location.

A third type of medical-related fraud occurs when a patient steals a handful of prescription forms, then attempts to forge prescriptions. This is a good reminder not to leave prescription pads or any other forgery-susceptible forms in the waiting room, examining room, or anywhere else that a patient might be alone with them.

Checklist: Medical Record-Keeping and Preventing Medical Fraud

1. Standard record-keeping procedures should be reviewed with staff periodically so that everyone contributing to the records will continue to follow correct and consistent practices.

2. Doctors and nurses should try to use the same pen during the day. This will eliminate confusion during infrared examinations of patient charts.

3. Make sure that your office receptionists know to have the patients themselves write their own names on sign-in sheets. This can help establish that the patient actually came in for a visit. Preserve these original sign-in sheets in a safe place in case you need them in the future.

4. Be consistent as to your procedure for the placement of hard stock behind the patient record on which you write.

5. Be consistent in your usage of patient record forms and prescription forms. Use offset-produced forms, as these are difficult to counterfeit.

6. Verify a patient's identity when he or she comes in for medical consultation or treatment.

7. Do not leave prescription pads or other forms in the waiting area or examination rooms where patients may take them.

ELEVEN

FRAUD IN THE INSURANCE AND BANKING INDUSTRIES

Safeguarding Financial Assets

I t is estimated that fraud in the insurance industry costs $120 billion per year. Of course, these costs are passed along to the consumer in the form of higher premiums. In the insurance industry, fraud can be perpetrated by the insured customer or by insurance agents and other company officials. Documents that come into question in the insurance industry can include applications for life, automobile, homeowners, renters, or supplemental insurance; earthquake and flood coverage; binders; driver exclusion agreements, and offers with signatures acknowledging acceptance or rejection of insurance.

The Six Types of Insurance Fraud

1. Fraud by arson

Of course, fraud by arson occurs when an insured torches his own house, business, or vehicle to collect the insurance money. There are flags that insurance investigators look for in the investigation of these cases. Was the insured heavily in debt or owing more on the property than what it was worth? Were there problems with county or city building personnel? Was there a divorce in which the spouse was awarded many of the household items and/or the property itself?

2. Fraud by theft of property

In this type of insurance fraud, the business owner or residential property owner breaks or sells his or her own possessions, then claims that they were stolen. In other cases, such possessions may never have been owned by the insured, and they produce bogus receipts to back up their bogus claims.

A man who owned a restaurant in California filed a false property loss claim with an insurance company. He created bogus receipts for expensive restaurant equipment he had supposedly bought in Chicago. First of all, the Chicago vendor could not be located by the insurance carrier's investigator, showing that this company was fictitious. Second, the sales receipt for the items purchased was handwritten in the hand of the insured, who was also the purchaser. Of course, one would expect that such an itemized sales receipt would normally be filled out by the company employee who is selling the equipment, not by the buyer. Demonstrating that the receipt was filled out in the insured's handwriting proved the claim was bogus, enabling the insurance company to deny it.

When the insured cannot produce receipts, then investigators seek information as to where the items were lost or stolen and where they were purchased. That is, they may check with the stores for any records of alleged purchases by the insured. In these cases bogus documentation may appear to substantiate claims, including bogus statements by people who later cannot be found to back up the statements. In this regard, all receipts and loss-substantiating documents that are submitted by the insured need to be authenticated.

3. Fraud by theft or destruction of a vehicle or marine vessel

This type of fraud is often carried out through arson or through an intentional accident in which the vehicle is totaled. In the case of the marine vessel, it may be intentionally sunk. In this type of fraud, the investigator needs to have all documents examined to see if all signatures match, starting with the insurance application. Red flags would be indicated by the following circumstances: Was the insured behind in payments? Did the insured take out the policy recently? Is there any record that the insured was trying to sell the vehicle or vessel just before the incident in question?

4. Fraud by phony bodily injury claims

There are two types of fraud in bodily injury claims. One is outright fraud in which the insured, a doctor, and an attorney are all involved. In these cases, all the medical treatment is on paper only. The doctor states that he has treated a person, usually for soft tissue injury, and charges huge fees. The attorney then takes the claim to the insurance carrier. This type of fraud is often carried out by four or five people in one vehicle who create an accident. The occupants are usually paid $100 each by a middle man who stages the accident, instructing the participants what their respective roles are to be. The occupants give the police their names and tell the police they will seek their own doctor. All subsequent treatment turns out to be on paper only.

To investigate this fraud, all documents with the alleged signatures need to be analyzed, including the sign-in sheets that are at the doctor's offices. It may be discovered that the different victims of the car accident have never actually gone to the doctor's office. Instead, the doctor or one of his staff simply fills out sign-in sheets and creates bogus medical charts to substantiate the billings to the insurance carriers.

The other type of bodily-injury fraud is called quasi fraud. Here the claimant builds up his medical bills just to get a larger settlement. The same handwriting and signature examinations mentioned above should be conducted on all documents pertaining to this matter to determine who is really preparing and signing the paperwork. It may be just a matter of a patient seeing the physician more often than is really necessary, but the physician cooperates on his end so as to continue receiving money for services rendered.

5. Fraud by the insurance agent

Not all insurance fraud involves the insured trying to rip off the insurance company. In many cases I have worked, insurance agents or their supervisors have been the ones who forged documents in an effort to cover mistakes in the original policy or to deny claims by the insured.

An insurance agent or insurance company official might forge documents, such as cancellation requests by insured parties, in an effort to deny claims by the insured. The agent might claim that the insured had previously canceled the policy before the theft, fire, or whatever occurrence leading to the claim. In such a case, the signature on the cancellation request should be compared with true samples of the insured's signature to determine whether or not the signature on the request was forged.

6. Fraud by bogus insurance companies

In this type of fraud, insurance companies from other countries, mostly in South America, advertise cheap insurance. The problem is that when the insured has a claim, the company has either vanished or simply will not honor the claim. If you have not heard of a particular company, you should contact the insurance commission to verify its validity in your state. You certainly should not take out insurance for domestic purposes with companies outside of the United States.

Bogus Claims and the Importance of Documentation

Any of the handwritten, typewritten, signed, or initialed entries, including checkmarks, on insurance documents can come into dispute. Many of the matters discussed in Chapter 4, Contract Fraud, can also be applied to insurance policies and related documents.

If you are an insurance agent, when filling out a specific policy with boxes to check or with circles or Xs or initials in certain places, you should use one pen to fill out everything. If you use a different pen to fill out a few parts of the policy, it could later be alleged that you filled the disputed part out after the insured parties left and without their knowledge or consent. I worked one such case where the only dispute about the document was whether or not a couple of Xs were truly part of the original policy.

As the agent, you should always try to keep the original policies and related documents if at all possible. Your original documents will vindicate you should any disputes arise with the insured in the future. For example, if they claim that you forged their signatures, or particularly if they claim that you did a cut and paste forgery of their signatures on the document, the availability of the original document will dismiss this claim in short order. The probative value of original ink on paper is one of the most powerful forms of evidence in such cases.

Another thing that insurance companies have to watch out for is claimants denying receipt of checks which have been issued to pay for claims. Many times a claimant, after endorsing an insurance check, contacts the insurance carrier and tells him that the check was never received.

In these cases the most obvious place to begin an investigation as to the validity of such a claim is with an examination of the endorsement signature on the check.

Following the money may only lead to dead ends, as the claimant would not deposit such a check into his own account. Instead he might simply cash the check against the carrier's bank or deposit it in a fictitious account. There are different avenues of investigation to pursue, but suffice it to say that it would be a good policy for the insurance company to keep original canceled checks for a couple of years until such matters are well settled.

As the insured customer, whenever you take out an insurance policy, you should also keep copies of the policy. If you fill out any changes to the policy or fill out any other documents that pertain to the original policy, you should obtain copies of these as well. If a dispute should arise about the validity of documents, your best defense will be the copies that you have retained. Keep those copies you receive (usually NCR copies, meaning No Carbons Required), as well as policies, amendments to policies, and other correspondence from your insurance agent. You should request that any matters discussed on the phone be put into writing; don't proceed on the basis of assumptions from phone conversations with your agent.

Checklists: Insurance Fraud Prevention

For the Insurance Company:

1. Insurance agents should use the same pen to fill out all the forms pertaining to a particular client.

2. Keep the original policies and related documents. If a claim comes into question, consider the following:

   1. Can it be demonstrated that the policy was taken out recently?

   2. Do the receipts and other loss-substantiating documentation by the insured make sense and seem legitimate?

   3. Can you locate the supposed signers of any statements? Will they substantiate their written statement, or were these statements really made in the hand of the insured?

4. For bodily injury claims, can you confirm through documentation that the injured actually went to see the doctor?

For the Policy Holders:

1. When you take out any new insurance policy, keep copies of all insurance documents, especially those containing your signatures and initials. If an agent is going to defraud a customer, these documents will contain the resources from which to forge signatures.

2. Start a separate file for that insurance policy, and keep all documentation together for that policy. When follow-up docments come in the mail, add them to the file.

3. Any matters discussed on the phone with the agent should be included in the policy or in an addendum.

4. Do not take out insurance for domestic purposes with companies outside of the United States.

Fraud in the Banking Industry

Banking-related fraud may attack from outside the walls of the bank, or its origin may be the bank employees inside. Your bank tellers are the sentries at their posts to prevent fraud when it comes from outside the bank. The managers and supervisors are the ones who will guard against internal embezzlements by bank employees.

External Fraud

External banking fraud is perpetrated both by regular bank customers who get in over their heads financially, and by rip-off artists who may open up a bank account for a short time as a tool for his scam. Perhaps the most common banking scam known to the public is the check kiting scam. If you can visualize a person flying a kite, as he lets out more string, the kite rises higher and higher. In check kiting, an account balance is artificially inflated with check deposits from other accounts that have no money behind them.

While the system is a day or two behind verifying deposits, the ATM machine thinks that there is ample money in the account, so it will release funds to the person who is withdrawing cash. Some people don't realize that there is a little camera in the ATM taking their picture; other more savvy operators know this, but don't care since they will be two states away by the time the bank catches the problem.

Some fraud is perpetrated inadvertently by account holders who formerly were good customers. These are people who are having financial problems and are trying to find a way out. Check kiting is one method that these account holders might use. It may not start intentionally, but after they find out that they can get away with it, they just continue allowing their bank to provide them with unauthorized loans.

In a different example of a customer getting in over his head and looking for a way out, a bank customer was gambling overseas. He cashed $30,000 against his VISA credit account and proceeded to lose the money gambling. When he arrived back in the United States, he contacted his credit card company and claimed that his credit card had been stolen and that someone else had used his card to charge up the $30,000. A bank representative contacted me to perform an examination of the signature on this single credit slip. His signature was shown to be authentic, proving that the account holder himself was the person who had authorized the withdrawal of these funds. Consequently, the bank held the customer to the obligation against his account.

Fraud may occur either outside the bank or right at the teller's window. It is interesting to find that some tellers do not pay attention to what is happening at their windows. For example, some tellers have cashed stolen checks that have been altered using white-out. Upon removing portions of the white-out, the true account holder's name was revealed underneath. Remember: if a document appears bogus, it probably is.

Loan Scams

Another type of banking scam concerns banks or loan institutions that make business or personal home loans. There are two types of scams that can be committed against the loaning institution. In the first type, after the business or home owner receives the check for the loan, he will cash it at the loan institution's bank, showing little to no identification or a phony identification. For that matter, he could try to have a third party cash the check. Later, he will deny that he ever received the funds, or he might contend that he lost it and did not have the opportunity to deposit it, arguing that his endorsement was forged.

A variation to the preceding scam occurs when the recipient of the loan denies ever having signed any of the loan documents. This is an absurd claim since the person would have filled out application forms and other loan documents, including a promissory note, and perhaps some of the signatures would have even been notarized. However, to resolve this dispute it would be necessary to go through the motions of proof. A simple handwriting and signature comparison would be necessary to show that the applicant really did fill out and sign the loan application and other related loan documents.

Securities and Investment Frauds

It is not very difficult for a smooth-talking scammer to gather together two million dollars as seed money to begin a Ponzi scheme, described in more detail in Chapter 13. Once the scam artist deposits funds and develops a rapport with a bank manager, he then requests a letter that describes an understanding between the bank and this customer that the two million dollars will remain on account for at least a year. This letter becomes part of the portfolio used by the scamming promoter to demonstrate stability and encourage others to invest in the program. What begins to happen with this account is that large amounts of money come in, while small checks go out as the supposed interest payments to the investors. This is a clue to the banker that a Ponzi scheme may be in progress.

New Account Scams

When opening new accounts, there are precautions that should be taken to deter fraud. When a banker receives a new account application, he should verify that all the information given is accurate. That means calling home, work, and reference telephone numbers. It is very common for a scammer to use a cell phone, fax number, or made-up number as his home or work number. It is also common for him to use a P.O. box or suite number for his address. These are all red flags. The bank employee should never deviate from established bank policies and procedures when opening a new account.

There is another popular scheme in which scammers open up bank accounts on the strength of counterfeited military identifications. When the account crashes, there is no way to follow up on these people. Bank employees should be wary of opening accounts using only military identifications; be sure to obtain multiple identifications. Further, get a good photocopy of the military identification photograph. Otherwise, you will have nothing to go on if you need to pursue an account holder who has scammed the bank.

Merchant Fraud Against the Bank

In this scheme, the scammer opens a merchant account at a bank, and he may even set up a store front to make sure he qualifies for such an account. This new merchant then debits stolen credit cards, depositing the money into his merchant account. He may also offer a service or product to entice people to place orders, but he does not fill them. On the surface, everything seems OK for about five months. Meanwhile, the scammer systematically withdraws money from his account in various ways, including withdrawing cash from ATM machines; making point of sale (debit card) purchases against his merchant account; writing checks against the account, and making cash withdrawals at the bank.

The cardholding victims have not received their goods and services, however, so they begin to dispute the transactions. When they do, their credit card issuers request proof of transactions from the bogus merchant. He ignores these notices when they come in the mail, knowing full well that he has at least 45 days before the actual charge-backs will come through.

When the items are finally charged back, the bank must now honor the charge-backs and debit the scammer's merchant account. The problem is that this scammer's account no longer has sufficient funds to cover the charge-backs. Consequently, the bank is left with the financial obligation and has now become the victim. The scammer, meanwhile, has timed things properly and is long gone.

Bankers can protect against this type of scam by monitoring the activity of merchant accounts. For example, if $60,000 is coming into an account monthly on ACH transactions (Automated Clearing House or paperless transactions), make sure that the account's balances are going up rather than down. Make sure there are not large numbers of NSF (Non Sufficient Funds) check items or large individual withdrawals.

Essentially, those bent on committing fraud have convenience technology, multiple identities, elaborate schemes, no morals, and leaky stories. The bank employee has access to information, a need to build a client base, client data, internal help (policies, procedures, manuals, supervisors), and policy restrictions for new accounts. It is the bank vs. the bad guys. Use the tools you're given!

The Inkless Fingerprint Program: a Deterrent to External Banking Fraud

If your bank or loan institution has not yet implemented the inkless fingerprint program, you should consider doing so. It can save your institution thousands of dollars by preventing fraud before it occurs, or by providing identification information for later investigations. In some areas this is known as the Fraud Deterrent Thumb Printing Program. The program is twofold. First, it is announced to the consumer through window and countertop stickers that are placed in plain view. This in itself can discourage a person from even attempting to pass a worthless check.

The second aspect of the program is to actually have the consumers place their thumbprints on negotiable instruments using the inkless inkpad, which actually is a small pad of ink. The term "inkless" is a misnomer because the ink itself and the thumbprint it produces are visible. However, it is called inkless because after being used to make a thumbprint on a check, the residual ink will simply disappear when the customer wipes the thumb on the palm of the other hand.

In the past some banks have not wanted to request fingerprints from customers since this may upset some of their good customers. More and more banks, however, have implemented the inkless fingerprint program, and I believe that the public has become more accustomed to the idea that they may have to give away a fingerprint from time to time.

Loan Scams and Bogus Bankers

Another type of banking-related fraud that victimizes the customer is the advance fee scam, which defrauds a person who is seeking a loan or other financial benefit. This victim may have credit problems, be unqualified for the loan sought, or need more funds than would otherwise be available to him in his present financial situation. This victim may end up dealing with a con man who requires an advance fee as a prerequisite to obtaining the otherwise untouchable loan. This banker may represent himself as a loan officer of a local bank, or he may claim he is the representative of private investors. Promises are made that the loan will be approved, but first the advance fee must be collected from the victim. The victim pays the fee in the hope of getting the loan, but after he pays it, the suspect absconds with the money and is never heard from again.

During desperate times (which we have all been through), our temptation is to dispense with precautionary measures in the hope of finding quick solutions to our problems. Resist temptations to shortcut common sense measures. Find solutions through reputable channels instead.

Internal Bank Fraud

This occurs when bank employees rip off their very own bank customers, or they rip off the bank itself. There are three primary reasons why internal bank fraud occurs:

1. The need or motivation of the employee.

2. The ability of the employee to rationalize the fraud, i.e. "The bank has billions of dollars that they'll never miss," or "They don't need this $10,000 as much as I do," or "The bank treats me badly," etc.

3. The bank's limited tools for prevention and/or detection.

Most employees don't intend to commit fraud, but circumstances sometimes push them into acting out of desperation. Complacent management, control breakdowns, decreasing quality and loyalty of employees, and a high dollar return vs. moderate risk are all additional factors in the increase of internal bank fraud.

Fraud Against Bank Customers

One case involved a receptionist who worked in a doctor's office and her husband who worked at a bank. When one of the doctor's patients gave a check for services to the receptionist, she phoned the account number of the check to her husband. He then set up a series of withdrawals from that account to pay for expenses that this banker and his wife had racked up against their American Express card to the tune of $300,000.

In another example, a teller at a bank in Portland forged a series of counter checks from a customer's account, making them payable to her roommate. The roommate then deposited these checks to her account at another bank. Once the funds cleared, this roommate then withdrew the funds in cash. It took quite some time for the fraud to be discovered because the victim was elderly and did not keep a very close eye on her monthly bank statements.

The employment application of this teller became instrumental in proving that she was the person who forged these checks. This employment application was lengthy, requiring the applicant to answer a lot of questions. Many times it becomes a hopeless cause to attempt to compare writings by a suspected employee when his or her file contains very little handwriting specimen materials. For this reason, banks should ensure that the employment application process demand that the applicant fill out a good number of materials, including several handwriting exemplar forms.

There are many other instances of bank employees ripping off their own customers. Further, many of these employees also answer phones at the bank, so they are able to cover their tracks when the customer calls to complain about the problem by simply taking the call themselves. To prevent this, customers should be given a special number to call when there are problems with their accounts. That number should ring at the manager's desk.

Customers should also be instructed that the best way for them to protect themselves against possible fraud is to balance their personal and business bank statements every month when they arrive. This will reveal whether or not fraud is being committed against them in the form of check-card rip-offs, embezzlements, mail fraud, or fraud committed against them by bank employees.

Checklists: Preventing Banking-Related Fraud

External Banking Fraud Prevention:

1. Do not open customer accounts on the basis of only a military identification. These are routinely counterfeited.

2. Do not open an account on the basis of any one piece of identification. There must be at least two pieces of government-issued or state-recognized identification.

3. Make sure your new accounts personnel are thorough in filling out new account application forms and bank signature cards.

4. Tellers should not accept checks that have been whited out.

5. Consider using an inkless fingerprint program. This can deter much fraud since those intending to commit fraud do not want to give away a fingerprint.

Internal Banking Fraud Prevention:

1. When customers sign up for new accounts, a special phone number to call when there are problems with their account should be included in the information given them. This special number should ring at the manager's desk.

2. Surveillance cameras that are positioned to record activity at all tellers' windows and desks would discourage employees from attempting to commit fraud against the bank and bank customers.

3. Ensure that employment application packets contain numerous documents that must be filled out by the employee. It would also help to include handwriting exemplar forms that repeat the format and text of everyday checks and other typical banking documents.

TWELVE

REAL ESTATE AND PROBATE DOCUMENTS

Deeds, Wills, and Forgeries

I have found that when it comes to real estate and probate, the average person does not fully understand the documents involved. If you were to ask five people to describe and explain the nature and purpose of the documents they signed when they purchased their first home, I'll bet that perhaps only one person could accurately do so. The same could be said of probate documents. So we will begin each section of this chapter by describing the nuts and bolts of real estate and probate documents before discussing forgery and fraud in these areas.

Real Estate Documents

In the fast-paced world of real estate, when the right deal presents itself, buyers must act quickly. With purchase agreements and addendum forms onboard the mobile office, offers and counteroffers are handwritten, signatures are affixed, and copies are exchanged. Changes are made in the form of interlineations, cross-outs, additions, and corrections. With buyers, sellers, agents, and brokers all involved in the process, this is a profit/loss-charged environment that is ripe for trouble. Disputes sometimes leading to litigation or arbitration can arise over real estate documents when people sign them in a rush, make incorrect assumptions about the deal, make mistakes in drawing up the documents, or even intentionally commit fraud.

With this in mind, all parties participating, particularly agents and brokers who fill out contracts every week, should exercise diligence in complying with proper protocol when filling out purchase agreements and other real estate documents. Even though time is of the essence, you should allow for enough time to go through the entire contract, talk through everything with the buyers and sellers, and make sure you dot your I's and cross your T's. Review Chapter 4 on Contract Fraud as a refresher before you draw up your next agreement, and observe the following recommendations:

Don't be in a rush!

The first mistake that people often make during a real estate transaction is signing documents without giving complete thought to the agreements. After looking at thirty properties, the buyers have finally decided on their perfect home. Perhaps they are so frustrated and worn out from all of their real estate browsing that they now don't give complete attention to the agreement at hand. They just want to sign the papers and get it over with.

Likewise, the sellers have been waiting for a long time, or perhaps they need to move on to that new home or new job, and they are therefore not as focused on the legal paperwork as they should be. Even the agents can be in a hurry to seal the deal before one or more of the parties change their minds or their situation. But agents, buyers, and sellers all need to take their time going through the documents to make sure that everything is understood, that all of their questions are answered, and that the purchase agreement, addendums, and disclosures all represent fully their intent and desires for the property transaction.

Don't make incorrect assumptions.

This is a common problem. The buyers assumed that the roof, the plumbing, or the fence were to be repaired. The seller assumed that the buyer was to deposit $3,000 instead of $1,000 into escrow. The buyer's agent assumed that his client would pay certain points. Everything that is assumed about a transaction should be written down on a tablet of paper as a checklist, and then when the formal documents are to be prepared, these issues should be addressed and incorporated into the written documentation.

Understand the real estate documentation.

Many people buying or selling a home don't understand the paperwork, and they blindly trust their agent to do everything properly and to make sure that their interests are incorporated into the documentation. To ensure that they understand all aspects of the process, however, buyers and sellers should sit down with their agents and ask them a lot of questions, such as, "What does this mean here?" or "Where does the contract discuss the pest inspection report?" It's far better to ask many seemingly stupid questions now than to try to fix issues that were written down incorrectly or not at all.

Here are the highlights of the more important real estate documents. All of these documents should be filed with your local County Recorder's office. A *grant deed* transfers ownership of the property to another person. It may be transferred as a gift between family members, or some financial consideration may be involved. When a grant deed is executed, the transfer is complete, all payments have been satisfied, and the deal is done. There are no loose ends or provisions that need to be met.

A *deed of trust,* or trust deed, also transfers the property from the former owner to the new owners. In this situation, the new owners only make a partial payment, the down payment, but a lending institution pays the remaining balance, thus satisfying the former owner so that he will release title to the property. In order to guarantee that the new owners continue making the agreed payments to the lending institution, a promissory note is completed wherein the borrowers promise to make the monthly payments on time until the loan is paid in full. The property is used as collateral to ensure that the new owners will continue to make those payments. The promissory note is referenced in the deed of trust. These documents are recorded at the same time, and this recording marks the close of escrow. Preparing and filing all of these documents with the County Recorder's office is the job of the title company in many states. In some states, an attorney's office will serve in this capacity.

When the last payment is finally made to the lending institution, the reconveyance is completed and also filed with the county recorder. The reconveyance is the document that states that the promissory note has been paid in full and the holder of the note, or beneficiary, no longer has the right to use the property as collateral to ensure payments on the promissory note. This is what people mean when they say, "We paid off the note on the house."

Direct Real Estate Transactions (without Broker or Agent)

In many states there is no law that says a person must use a real estate broker or real estate agent to buy or sell real property. I have personally purchased and sold many homes without going through realtors and brokers. Although this can be risky business, to those of us who are meticulous by nature and who understand documents, it can work. Although the real estate transactions I have made this way have worked out fine, there are still some dangers that must be avoided.

Many people are unaware that when a title insurance company issues title insurance on the home you have purchased, they are only insuring against recorded deeds of trust. This is significant for two reasons. First, you can go down to the local county recorder's office yourself and find out what's against the property as long as you understand what all the documents mean. For example, you would need to understand the ingredients to a basic deed, what a reconveyance is, and how to fill them out so that they can be properly recorded.

Second, the possibility exists that there could be some deed floating around out there that was never recorded. For example, let's say that you and I strike a deal regarding the transfer of your home. I agree to pay you $200,000 for your home. I draw up the grant deed, which says that for value received, you are granting me your home. I give you the 200K, you move out, and I move in. It can be that easy. Although there would be property tax implications in this scenario, I could just hang on to that deed and not record it. I could live in the home for many years, and anyone checking on the status of the property in question at the local recorder's office will just see your name as owner of the property.

The more likely scenario occurs when a person uses the equity in his or her home as security for a second mortgage to obtain a loan. In this case there is a promissory note and a second trust deed to back up that promissory note, and that is why this procedure is called taking out a second mortgage. This trust deed now stands in second position behind the first. That is, the first deed has legal priority to be paid off first in the event of foreclosure or sale of the property and if there is any money left over, then the second deed will be paid. It is fairly common that these second trust deeds among family members and friends are not recorded at the local county recorder's office. There is no law that says that they must be recorded, but recording them is the smart thing to do.

The deals just described were all legitimate, but what follows was not. Now we come to the sometimes ugly side of real estate, where in the dark shadows truly unscrupulous vultures lie in wait for the opportunities that present themselves upon the occasion of death. There was a woman living with an elderly man. Upon his death, she found a copy of his escrow papers in a file and created a grant deed wherein the already deceased man supposedly deeded the property over to her. Of course, she backdated the deed to several months prior to his death, forged his signature, and counterfeited a notary stamp. She squatted on the property on the strength of this deed and would not allow the deceased man's children in to go through his personal possessions.

In her audacity and to hold the children at bay, she came to me to authenticate the deed. She provided me samples of the deceased man's signatures, but she also inadvertently slipped in some samples of her own writing when she passed the documents on to me. Upon my review of the documents, I determined not only that the deceased man was not the person who had signed the deed, but also that my client herself was the person who had forged his name.

Fraud Issues in Real Estate

As seen in the above example, fraud is an issue that sometimes emerges after the property has gone through escrow, or even later. For any number of reasons, someone is now unhappy with a real estate deal and decides to fix it by correcting his or her copy of the real estate documents, or by fabricating bogus ones. In my practice, I have seen fraud committed by buyers, sellers, agents, and brokers, not to mention the scam artists and their techniques.

One case brought in from the California State Department of Real Estate involved the investigation of a broker who had agreed to handle a real estate transaction as a return favor for a client. When the buyer signed the purchase agreement, the commission line was blank. Sometime later, the broker decided to change the deal and wrote in 3% on the commission line. When the buyer discovered this, he became upset, and the issue moved beyond the money when the buyer turned the broker in to the Department of Real Estate. When confronted with this story during the investigation, the broker denied altering the agreement. An agent with the Department of Real Estate brought me the purchase agreement to examine it for signs of tampering.

At first glance, the entire agreement was in black ink and appeared to have been filled out in its entirety with the same pen. However, when I viewed the document under infrared examination, all the ink on the document responded consistently to changes in infrared barrier filters except for the questioned entry of 3%. While the main body of ink disappeared at a lower wavelength, the questioned 3% entry continued to be visible throughout the higher spectrum of infrared light. Such a variation proves that the two inks are different. This confirmed that the pen used to make the commission entry was not the same one used to fill out the remainder of the form in the buyer's presence, suggesting that the document had been altered.

Caution: be sure to use the same pen for all of the handwriting, signatures, initials, additions, and corrections on a real estate document. Also, be sure to keep your best copies of listing and purchase agreements, addendums, leases, and other documents.

Meta-escrow Fraud

These are the frauds perpetrated down the road that really have nothing to do with the original real estate transaction documents or escrow paperwork. For example, deeds are commonly forged by spouses who are going through a divorce. In this scenario, the spouse who has control of the property forges the name of the soon-to-be ex-spouse. He or she may also counterfeit a notary's stamp and affidavit, then record the documents.

Keep in mind that when you record a document at the county recorder's office, the recorder is only concerned as to the proper form of the document and does not verify the information on the grant deed. If all of the blank spaces have been filled in and if the document appears to be in order, then the clerk will record it. After the fraud-minded spouse records the property, he or she either encumbers it with a second loan and takes the money, allowing the house to go into foreclosure, or simply sells the property quickly and keeps the proceeds.

Real Estate Fraud by Scam Artists

Sometimes a scam artist will make forcible entry into a house that is up for sale, change the locks, then rent it to an unsuspecting person. The suspect usually gives the victim a bogus lease with a forged signature of the homeowner. With the first and last month's rent, along with a deposit, the scammer makes quite a bit of money for a day's work. If you doubt the integrity of the person offering a house for rent, describe to a neighbor the person who is offering the house for lease, and see if he or she can confirm that the description matches that of the true owner.

There are also scam artists who will contact people who are losing their home due to being behind in their mortgage payments. The scam artist tells the victim that if he or she signs the grant deed over to him, he will solve the problem. The scam artist tells the victim he needs $500 for all of the paperwork, and the victim gives the scammer the money and signs the grant deed over to him.

Although the victim feels as though he has been relieved from a foreclosure, he has not carefully read the contract that he has signed, which states that the scammer is not responsible for any mortgages. The victim next receives a notice from the mortgage company that it is foreclosing. This is when the victim first realizes that he has been taken. He is now far behind in his mortgage payments; he has also signed his interest away, and when the bank forecloses, it goes on the victim's credit record.

People don't have to be professional scam artists to try to get away with some audacious real estate scams. Three sisters all signed loan documentation to refinance a home they owned together. They later agreed to lie about the loan so they wouldn't have to pay back the money they had received. They came up with the story that they did not endorse the check issued to them on the new loan, nor did they sign the title documents (including their signatures in the notary's log), nor did they sign the loan application form. When I examined these documents, it was quite obvious that these three sisters had indeed made all of their supposedly forged signatures on these documents. This was just another case of legitimate contract denial as discussed in Chapter 4.

Since these types of fraud cases are so prevalent in real estate documents, I advise the following precautions:

Checklist: Preparing and Securing Real Estate Transactions

1. Ask a local title company for a preliminary title report on the property you are thinking about buying. This takes only a few hours to get and can even be faxed to you. It will tell you the owner of record for that property.

2. Contact the State Department of Real Estate to check up on realtors and brokers if you have any reservations about the people with whom you are doing business.

3. Check with the property neighbors to confirm the description of the property owner who is offering the property for sale or lease.

4. Do not be in a rush. Allow time to give proper thought to the deal and to prepare all documents properly.

5. Do not make assumptions. Include all aspects of the transaction in the written contract. Make sure you have read and understood the entire agreement.

6. Use the same pen to write all of the signatures, dates, addresses, and initials on a single contract.

7. Keep the best copies available to you of listing and purchase agreements, addendums, leases, and all other documents. Insist that you have a copy of any document that is signed by the parties.

8. Lock all escrow and title documents in a safe-deposit box and inform the executor of your will of the safe box number and bank location. Do not leave these documents sitting around your home.

9. Review Chapter 4 on contract fraud before drawing up or signing your next agreement.

10. Draw up an ironclad will that details what is supposed to happen to your real estate upon your death. Tell your family and loved ones your desires for your real estate and personal property, so that everyone knows what's supposed to happen with your property when you are gone.

Of course, your real property is just one part of your estate. In the following section we will discuss probate fraud and some measures that you can take to protect the integrity of your entire estate.

Probate Issues

Wills are loaded with traditions that relate back to common law in England. There are some features of wills that are timeless and universal, and rightly so. It is important that a will be universal and timeless because a will prepared in New York in 1925 should still be valid and recognized in Los Angeles in the year 2002. Can you imagine the confusion and havoc of trying to probate a will in one state that had different probate laws than the state in which the will was written?

I have already offered some advice in the previous section about how to safeguard your real property. We will complete that discussion in this section on probate fraud, but before I proceed, I just want to remind you that I am not an attorney and I do not presume to be practicing law. The advice that I give in these chapters comes from my personal experience and involvement in cases as a Questioned Document Examiner, and that is the perspective from which I speak.

Probate has to do with documents surrounding a person's death. It involves the distribution of what the deceased has left behind, which might include income-producing businesses, cash from insurance policies, real property, bank accounts, and stock portfolios, as well as any valuable personal property, such as works of art or collectibles. I work at least one probate-related case each week. Bogus wills, codicils, trusts, deeds, designations of beneficiaries, and contracts seem to come out of the woodwork when people die. Such documents may be out-and-out forgeries, or they may have been altered or have missing and/or substituted pages. The motivation, of course, is that there are usually a lot of assets at stake when it comes to probate matters.

Intriguing issues emerge in probate documents. New designations of beneficiaries may have been legitimately signed just prior to death, or they may have been forged. New bank accounts may have been established with new signature cards that become questioned. There are a lot of matters to think about when a person approaches death. While some prepare for it thoughtfully, in an atmosphere of calm, others do it amidst squabbling vultures, knowing that brewing tensions will erupt into all-out war once the patriarch or matriarch dies.

But whether in an atmosphere of calm or under pressure from family members, documents are prepared and signed. Many are those who sign documents in failing health with the little strength and motor control they have left. When examining documents prepared under such circumstances, questions emerge such as, Is this the authentic tremor of failing health? Or is it the tremor of forgery? These matters can be sorted out by the professional Questioned Documents Expert.

In one example of a probate dispute, the mother of four siblings died in-testate (without leaving a will). One of the siblings squatted on the property and consorted with a Notary Public to forge a grant deed, which he used to obtain a loan on the property. He also forged his late mother's name to a transfer of ownership document, thus taking possession of a mobile home.

By forging these documents, this sole brother was able to take possession of the majority of the assets left by the mother. Of course, the remaining siblings took issue with this brother and challenged the deed in court. A complication in the litigation was that the mother had remarried and her surname had changed, so it was difficult to obtain true handwriting samples of the deceased under the name which appeared on this questioned deed. However, a diligent search did yield the proper documents to resolve the matter.

When the Notary Public was called as a witness, she testified that she had lost all of the records pertaining to this deed, but she maintained her story that she had known the deceased and had witnessed her sign the document fourteen years earlier. The squatter's attorney was very skilled in his questions, tactics, and case strategy. In the final analysis, however, the judge ruled that even he was able to see the fundamental differences between the questioned signature on the deed and the true signature samples by the deceased. The judge ruled in favor of the plaintiffs (the remaining siblings), and the day's end found all of these adult siblings visiting with each other and beginning to restore communication. One of the four plaintiffs told me, "I hadn't spoken to Johnny in five years."

It was nice to see the beginnings of healing in this family, but so many times, the ending is not so happy. Rather, family members try to cut one another out of the estate by conniving, forging, and tweaking documents. It always amazes me that at the time when family should be supporting and consoling one another, they are sometimes at each other's throats with a vengeance. I will say that I have noticed a trend: the less prepared the estate, the greater opportunity for fraud and the more potential for bickering among the survivors.

Some common questions regarding the signatures on probate documents: Did the deceased really sign the deed or will? If it was not his or her genuine signature, then who was the forger? Was it the primary beneficiary? Was it a witness to the will? Were the witnesses' signatures, dates, and address information all written by the individual, legitimate witnesses, or were they really written by one and the same person? Known writing and signature samples of the deceased and the witnesses should be compared to see if they were truly written by these distinct persons.

Other questions may arise over the use of forms: Was a standard form used to prepare the will? If there is a form number on the document, was it a form consistent in time with the date that appears on the document? If there is a small form number that shows the form date to be 1995 (when the form itself was printed), but the questioned signature is dated in July of 1989, then you already know that the document was backdated. Little oversights on the part of the forger do occur, and such questions should be considered when evaluating the veracity of probate documents.

In a probate matter involving a gay couple, one of the partners died and left a will that bequeathed his estate to his partner. The family of the deceased contested the will, producing a phony will that cut out this partner. The decedent's signature was forged on this phony will, and on the witness attestation page that accompanied the bogus will, I discovered that the two witnesses' signatures and address information were all written by one person. One of the alleged witnesses could not be found, but the other witness refused to testify when the matter came before the probate judge. I testified, demonstrating that the decedent's signature had been forged and that the two witnesses' signatures and address information were all written by only one person.

Two Types of Wills

Holographic Wills

A holographic will is wholly in the handwriting or hand printing of the testator; there is no typing on it, and nobody else can write on a holographic document (instrument). It is dated and signed, and it expresses an intention that it serve as a will. Holographic wills should neither be notarized nor witnessed, in contrast to typewritten wills that require two witness signatures.

I have seen holographic wills written on scraps of paper, on writing tablets, and as the last pages of a letter to a family member. Although holographic wills are a neat idea, there are several potential landmines with such wills. The chief problem is likely to be that, since the will's content was handwritten by the testator, he or she probably did not obtain legal advice prior to drafting the document.

The biggest problem with holographic wills is their ambiguity. They were prepared by the testator, who probably did not think of everything that should have been addressed and who may not have used the clearest language to describe his wishes. Not only may the content of holographic wills be unclear, but there may also be other important issues that have been inadvertently overlooked by the writer. Another problem with this type of will is that the safety features that should be included in a will are not present. Since a holographic will can create so many kinds of probate-related difficulties, I advise getting an attorney to draw up your will for you.

Typewritten Wills

Typewritten wills are mechanically prepared by either a typewriter, or more likely, a computer printer. Typewritten wills must be signed by two different witnesses. These witnesses must be of legal age, they cannot be the beneficiaries of anything in the will, and they must sign according to the guidelines in the attestation clause. For example, if the attestation clause says that the witnesses witnessed each other signing the will, then that is supposed to be the case.

Prepare a will!

Many people avoid preparing a will because they either think there will be plenty of time to prepare one, or they just don't want to face the thought of death or deal with the unpleasantries of dividing up their life's work to leave behind. These are poor excuses. If you do not prepare an iron-clad will now, you don't know the heartache and trouble that may be in store for those who survive you. In the confusion after your death, your children, spouse, and close friends will wonder what your intentions really were.

If you have prepared a half-baked will to try to save legal fees, that just provides an opportunity for family, including step-family, to contest different aspects of the will or to contest its validity altogether. Having worked countless will disputes and having seen the frustration, alienation, and heated arguments of formerly docile family members, I advise you to prepare a will now if you have not done so. Have it written up by an attorney, and use the following guidelines for preparing and dealing with probate documents so that you can minimize the risk of confusion, bickering, or an out-and-out blitzkrieg of your estate after you are gone.

Remember that when a person dies, the family and friends who remain are usually not functioning at their best. The atmosphere surrounding a person's death can be volatile, with many different emotions running rampant. Family members might say things to one another that they will later regret. You can help the situation by reducing issues to their minimums. If you make firm, clear decisions ahead of time, the family will most likely be inclined to abide by your wishes, not only as to who is to be the executor, but as to all the other issues that surround probate.

Make sure that you nominate an executor of your will and at least one alternate. This is the person who will administer your will. If you don't nominate the person you want as an executor, then you open the door for family members to argue over who is going to be the administrator of your estate. Furthermore, you should nominate an alternate as well in case the executor you nominate predeceases you.

I advise against a holographic will. Rather, your attorney should create your will using a computer word processing program such as Microsoft Word. Upon the completion of the will, he will provide you the original hard paper copy of the will with signatures. Request a copy of the floppy disk version of the file as well, and ask your attorney to maintain both a hard copy and a disk copy for his records. The purpose of this will be clear after reading Chapter 14, "Computer and Internet Fraud."

Where to Keep Your Will

Don't leave the original will at the house with your other paperwork. If you do, any person who finds it could destroy the original after using it for a template to create a will more to his own liking! Therefore, keep your original will and the floppy disk copy in a safe-deposit box to which you alone have a key, and leave one sealed copy with the executor and one sealed copy at your home. Inside these sealed envelopes you should include information as to where the original will is, including which bank and the safe-deposit box number. These sealed envelopes should be marked "WILL—To be opened upon the event of my death." You can tell family and friends highlights of your will ahead of time, but they don't need to know all the details, so make sure these copies are sealed.

Another good reason to keep the original will away from the house is that it adds a little extra measure of distance for those times when you might want to cut someone out of your will in the heat of emotion.

There was a man who had a heated argument with his adult son. After the son left, the father took the will from his closet, cut out this son from the will, and then returned it to the closet. Later, he patched things up with his son but forgot to correct the will. When the father died, this loving son suffered much grief and confusion when the estate was probated.

Contesting a Will

First of all, before attempting to contest a will, be sure that you have some good reason to challenge it. Being unhappy with the contents of the will is not enough grounds to attack it. But if you do have good cause to challenge a will, then you should retain an attorney and contact a Questioned Document Examiner. A trip to the probate court might be necessary for the QD Examiner to review the original will. This examiner should check the signatures of the testator and witnesses, check to see if the form falls within chronological considerations, and check for any evidence of alteration of pages or substituted pages.

Checklist: Preparing Your Will

1. Find an attorney to draw up your will. Don't allow family members or friends to push you into their wishes concerning your estate. An impartial attorney can provide you an invaluable service by drawing up a will that truly represents your wishes.

2. Prepare a will while you still have a clear mind and decent health.

3. Have the will witnessed by two adult, independent witnesses, following the guidelines in the attestation clause.

4. Review Chapter 4 on Contract Fraud to ensure you have incorporated safeguards into the preparation of your will.

5. I advise against a holographic will. Rather, your attorney should create your will using a computer word processing program such as Microsoft Word. Upon the completion of the will, he should provide you the hard copy original, with signatures, along with a floppy disk version of the file.

6. Do not leave the original will at the house with your other paperwork. Leave it in a safe-deposit box at the bank. Keep only one key for yourself, and don't include anyone else on the signature card. The executor can gain access to the safe box by producing a copy of your death certificate.

7. Leave copies of your will with the executor and at your house.

Checklist: Serving as an Executor

1. Review the points above with the person requesting your involvement so that he or she will know the precautions to take in preparing a will before it is handed over to you. If you are simply handed a will that has already been drawn up, you may later find yourself in the middle of disputing family members.

2. Make sure you have a good copy of all the will documents and also that you know where the will is kept.

3. When the testator dies, immediately locate the original will. Make a color copy of all the original will documents, then file the will with the local probate court.

4. When you clean out the decedent's papers, don't throw out any documents that have signatures on them. These seemingly insignificant documents might be critical in resolving any allegations of fraud that might be raised against the will.

CHAPTER THIRTEEN

AVOIDING PERSONAL AND INVESTMENT FRAUD

Hanging On to that Nest Egg

Ideally, your successful business has provided you the means to sock money away for retirement. Admittedly, all of us are always looking for new opportunities to leverage up our portfolios so that they provide us the maximum possible returns, whether we are in our income-earning years or in our retirement. However, that zeal can sucker us into some deals that could lose us everything we have accumulated. By reviewing the warnings and cautions in this chapter regularly, we stand far better chances of holding onto our wealth and retirement portfolios, so that we can enjoy the quality of life we have worked so hard to earn. I hope you will share these concepts with your family and friends.

An unscrupulous securities broker stole $95,000 from a ninety-year-old client. How did he manage such a thing? When the broker discovered that his client was in the hospital and not expected to survive, he typed up a letter, supposedly from his client, which instructed a financial services corporation to transfer all of the funds from the client's account to a third-party account. Of course, the broker had to forge the signature of his client on this letter.

The second part of this broker's scheme was to forge an Automatic Trade Settlement Authorization, giving control over the account to the broker. As it turned out, the elderly man survived, and two years went by before anyone found out what had happened. Since the man lived alone and hadn't told his family members about his assets, and since he had become senile, nobody missed the money. Oh, and it was a lousy forgery job to boot! The brokers scheme was finally uncovered, and he is now paying partial restitution.

This story points out the importance of keeping an eagle eye on your nest egg. You might have a very nice securities broker, but you should be careful how much control you give him or her over your finances. What follows are just some of the scams used by rip-off artists to transfer the resources of people just like you to their side of the balance sheets.

Identity Thefts

There are 500,000 cases of identity theft each year. In fact, the number is going up by about fifteen percent per year. It takes an average of two years to repair the damage, and many victims of identity theft feel that the police were not helpful in resolving their cases. Therefore, it is better to try to prevent identity theft than to try to clean up the mess after it happens. These thieves steal one or several important pieces of your personal information, such as your credit card number, driver's license number, or social security number, and use them in various ways. The following are some identity theft scams of which you should be aware.

Unauthorized Loans

A bookkeeper or even an outside source could use a copy of your financial statement to secure a loan against your business, then take the money and run. In this scam, the person uses your good name and good credit rating to establish a line of credit with a loan institution. When the crook receives the check for the loan, he cashes it and spends the money. You would not even know this had happened until the bank came looking for the first payment.

It's good to periodically check your personal and company credit reports with the various credit bureaus, just to see who is reporting what. You'll want to know if any unauthorized loans have been secured against your assets. Further, keep your personal information locked up. If a savvy bookkeeper knew what to do with only your date of birth (DOB) and your social security number, he or she could just about own you. If this information would somehow find its way into the garbage, dumpster divers could also own you.

Unauthorized Credit Cards

This topic has already been mentioned elsewhere, but it bears repeating here as an identity scam. It occurs when someone acquires a piece of your personal information, maybe from a lost wallet or from a pre-approved credit offer taken from your mail box or your garbage, then establishes credit in your name. Identity thieves can also swipe your credit card through a hand-held scanner, called a skimmer, to capture your personal information from the card strip. They then use this information to create fraudulent credit cards in your name. They can even use online software, which gives them step-by-step instructions on how to create phony identifications that combine your account information with the identity thief's photo and address. I myself have seen e-mail offers for such software.

These thieves open up credit accounts in your name, but they are careful to put their own mailing information on the applications so that the credit cards come to the crook instead of to you. When the cards arrive, the thieves have a heyday spending your money. It will be some time before you find out about this, and by then, the damage will already have been done. Then you will have problems getting loans, leasing equipment or cars, or doing other business because of this blemish on your credit report. It may take months—even a year to clear things up.

Internet Identity Fraud

Identity thieves may also use the Internet to gain information about you and/or to actually conduct the identity scam against you. An Internet identity scam may take many forms: The identity thief may pose as you and send your employer harassing e-mail messages against company officials, hoping to soil your reputation so that you do not receive a promotion. Or the thief may make Internet purchases or gamble on the Internet using your credit card account information.

Protect Yourself from Identity Fraud

To protect yourself from identity fraud, it is important to safeguard your personal information. You should always think twice before giving out your social security number, credit card numbers, driver's license number, home address, a copy of your birth certificate, your mother's maiden name, or even information about your stock accounts and other assets. When this information falls into the wrong hands, scammers can go to work unwinding your finances, stealing your possessions, and using your identity to leverage into further scams.

Because identity theft is becoming more common, the federal government has designated the Federal Trade Commission as the clearinghouse for victims. If you believe you have been the victim of an identity theft, you can file an online complaint with the FTC by going to http://www.consumer.gov/idtheft. This Internet site provides a wealth of information. In addition to filing an online complaint at this site, you should also file a police report with your local law enforcement agency.

There are a few things that you can do to eliminate or at least reduce the volume of those unsolicited credit offers that come to you in the mail. You will need to contact three credit reporting bureaus—Equifax, Experian, and Trans Union—and tell them you do not wish to receive pre-approved credit offers. You can do this with a single toll-free phone call to 1-888-5OPT-OUT. You may still get some of these, however, so be sure to shred them so they don't fall into the wrong hands.

You can also get off of junk mail and phone solicitation lists by signing up for the Direct Marketing Associations Mail Preference and Telephone Preference Services. You will have to do this with a letter. For the telephone service, the address is P.O. Box 9014, Farmingdale, N.Y. 11735-9014. The mail service address is P.O. Box 9008, Farmingdale, N.Y. 11735-9008.

If you need to contact the fraud divisions of Experian, Equifax or Trans Union, the numbers are: Equifax (800-525-6285), Experian (888-397-3742), and Trans Union (800-680-7289). If your social security number has been used fraudulently, report the problem to the Social Security Administration at 800-269-0271.

Checklist: Preventing Identity Theft

1. When establishing passwords and personal identification numbers (PINs), use obscure combinations of numbers and letters. Don't use any obvious information, such as the last four digits of your social security number, your birth date, portions of your phone numbers, or the numeric part of your address.

2. Try to never give your social security number to people who

ask for it. Offer other forms of identification if at all possible.

3. Check your credit reports periodically to make sure there are no surprises. Contact TWR, RCA, or Equifax, just to name a few. It costs a few dollars, but it's well worth it.

4. Get off of mailing lists for credit offers.

5. Clean out your wallet. Carry only things that you need and use frequently. Don't put your social security number in your wallet.

6. Close old checking and credit card accounts that you haven't used in awhile and don't really need.

7. Shred those credit offers when they come in the mail (did you get a shredding machine yet?).

8. When paying by credit card, always ask to swipe the card yourself. Servers are the most likely people to use a pocket-size skimmer; they have ample opportunity since they are frequently alone with a customer's card. Further, at filling stations or other places where you pay by credit card, don't leave your card with anyone who is out of your eyesight.

9. At a restaurant, do not lay your credit card on the table while waiting for the server to come by to get it. Someone may be watching, or even zooming in with a video camera, to capture customer's account numbers and expiration dates.

Telemarketing Scams

Please keep in mind that there are other scams out there besides paper scams.

Projected losses to telemarketing and direct personal marketing fraud schemes alone figure to be more than $40 billion annually. For example, there are many types of phone scams. A new variation to an old phone scam starts with a phone call to you. The caller claims that he or she is a representative of your bank and wants you, the customer, to cooperate with a test program. The caller then obtains your account number, credit card information, and/or social security number. After the call, the scam artist cleans out your bank account and maxes out your credit cards.

Never give out your social security number, bank information, credit card information, or any personal information to anybody who initiates a call to you. It's different if you call a company and use your credit card to order something. If a telemarketer calls you with an offer that interests you, you can request that he or she mail you paperwork regarding the offer. This will give you a better opportunity to consider if the offer is really legitimate, and it also gives you the added benefit of not buying something on impulse. If the telemarketer becomes pushy, trying to force you to make a purchase using your credit card, that should raise a red flag. Just terminate the conversation.

In another type of telephone fraud, an operator calls and informs the person who answers that there is a problem with the phone line. To make this scam seem believable, the caller may even use special sound effects to make it seem as if there truly is a problem with the phone line. The bogus operator then instructs the listener to dial a special number so that the problem can be fixed. Then the operator thanks the customer and hangs up, terminating the call, or so it would seem. In actuality, that special number that the customer dialed made an international connection that others were able to use to make overseas phone calls. The unsuspecting customer will scratch his head in wonder when he receives a phone bill showing thousands of dollars in overseas calls to mysterious phone numbers.

Avoiding this scam is simple. If you have a problem with your phone line, you will be the first one to know about it. In this situation, you will call the phone company to have them fix the problem; they will not call you to tell you about a problem that you have not yet experienced. If an operator calls you with such a request, hang up immediately.

Investment Schemes

There are many investment schemes out there in which investors are not getting what they believe they agreed to when they entered the deal. Remember, if something sounds too good to be true, it's probably a trap. Some examples:

Bogus Stock Transfers

In this scam, a phony company exchanges its worthless stock for the stock of a healthy company. The orchestrator of this scam creates bogus financial statements with inflated assets, then uses them to get other busi-nesses, like yours, to trade stock for a share of a bogus holding company. The assets of a legitimate company acquired in this way are then sold off or used as collateral on bank loans that are never paid. The best precau-tion when embarking on such transactions is to do your homework: verify the legitimacy and health of the company's stock you are considering.

West African (Nigerian) Scams

Over the past several years, Nigeria has gained a bad reputation in world business circles due to the activities of Nigerian syndicates who operate sophisticated fraud schemes on gullible foreign companies and individuals. These syndicates promise quick returns for cooperation in semi-legal business propositions. This is a $5 billion worldwide scam that has been going on now for about thirteen years. It is called the 419 Fraud, after the pertinent section of the Criminal Code of Nigeria. Most people in law enforcement agencies, especially in the larger cities, have seen these scams and know them to be a fact of life. Many people have lost large sums of money by falling victim to these scams because they are so excit-ing and believable. I should know—I was one of their targets.

I was contacted by these people via e-mail about nine months ago. I wanted to learn about the scam, so I played along and also researched it with each step. They sent me numerous formal documents regarding an oil deal that involved payments for bribes, international licensing agree-ments, bogus invoices, and formal national payment demands, among other documents. In fact, I have developed an entire file on this scam and use some of these documents in my seminars.

The appearance of these documents is very formal. The letter-head design, the stamp impressions, and even the content offer an air of au-thenticity. As my file of paperwork grew while I played along, I kept waiting for the other shoe to drop. I had to wait a long time. Whereas previously the various players in this scam had told me they were paying bribe money to move the deal along through the various stages, when the deal was close to culmination, they claimed they were now out of money, and they requested that I pay for the final bribe to culminate the deal. These are patient and provocative scammers, to be sure!

Of course, when they saw that I was not going to pay anything, they requested that I appear in their country to culminate the deal. I had also observed through research that our State Department is issuing warnings about U.S. citizens traveling to Nigeria. There is danger of being plundered, if not held for ransom, through involvement with these deals. Finally, when I saw they were losing interest in me, and just to torture them a bit more, I told them that I was related to Bill Gates. You should have seen the flurry of activity at that point! There were many phone calls and faxes urgently requesting my presence overseas.

These scams have several variations. The victims usually receive an unsolicited e-mail, fax, or letter from Nigeria, requesting help to launder money for nationals in high places in the oil industry, or they might even receive a seemingly legitimate business proposal by normal means. One scam has syndicates sending letters or faxes to businesses, inviting them to allow their bank accounts to be used for the temporary transfer of large sums of money, usually left over from abandoned government projects, in return for a 35% cut. The letters are signed by an individual who claims to be a highly placed official in the Nigerian National Petroleum Corporation (NNPC), the Central Bank of Nigeria, or some similar organization. Once access to the victim's bank account has been obtained, the scam artists then forge a transaction on the account, usually a request for an international money transfer to a third country, and the account is then emptied.

If the scammers do not succeed in liquidating the victim's banking accounts, they just move on to the next step of their master plan. At some point, the victim is asked to pay an advance fee as a bribe to culminate the deal or to satisfy a transfer tax, performance bond, etc. If the victim pays the fee, complications will follow that will require still more money, until the victim gets tired of throwing good money after bad. Alternately, the victim may be urgently requested to appear at Lagos, Nigeria, or some other destination to work out the deal. Don't do it! You may end up being kidnapped.

In another scam, foreign businesses are lured into sending thousands of dollars worth of goods to Nigeria, only to find that the check they are paid with is fraudulent; or that the bank it is drawn on does not exist; or that the money they thought had been transferred into their account has been transferred back out again; or that the money has come from an illegal source, such as another defrauded bank account in another country.

In a similar scheme, a team of Nigerians visited dealerships in the U.S. and purchased vast quantities of luxury cars, using worthless paper,

on a weekend, when banks were closed. They took possession immediately, drove them to a pier in San Francisco, then loaded all the vehicles
on a cargo ship that sailed off to Nigeria. By the time the U.S. car dealers
knew that they had been taken, the syndicate bosses were picking up
their new vehicles, which had been delivered to Port Harcourt, Nigeria!

The Nigerian syndicates also have their agents here in the U.S. working numerous other types of scams. They have a clear understanding of
how our banking systems work, and they operate many of the check scams
and negotiable instruments scams already mentioned in this book. For
example, there was an elaborate check-fraud ring that was arrested in Los
Angeles in June 2000. Nine people were charged, but others are believed
to still be out there working this scam. This group had stolen around
$400 million during the past four years.

These criminals targeted over one hundred victims, mostly businesses.
Federal investigators said that these businesses included MGM, Toyota,
Honda, Disney, Warner Bros., and Capitol Records. According to the
FBI, this counterfeiting and forgery syndicate mostly involved Nigerian
nationals living in the Los Angeles area. One of them was a former employee of the post office who orchestrated the stealing of checks and credit
cards from the businesses along his postal route.

In their highly organized scam, the checks were stolen, then forgers
would change the names of the payees and alter the amounts of the checks.
Afterwards, they deposited them into fictitious bank accounts, and through
those accounts the funds were converted to cashier's checks. One of the
stolen checks was made out to the King World production company from
Fox Television Stations. This stolen check was broken up into thirty-
three smaller checks.

The following warnings may sound harsh to you, but to those of us
who have worked these cases on the side of law enforcement, as well as to
the victims, these warnings are very much in order. By observing these
admonitions regarding any business dealings with Nigeria, you very well
may save your fortune or your retirement nest egg.

1.   Do not pay for anything up front, ever.

2.   Do not extend credit to any Nigerian official.

3.   Do not give them your checking account or credit card num-
     bers.

4. Do not travel to Nigeria or a neutral location, as you risk being kidnapped and held for ransom.

5. Be suspicious of negotiations regarding the Central Bank of Nigeria or the NNPC (Nigerian National Petroleum Corporation).

6. Do not expect that the Nigerian government will help you to recover your losses.

Fraud Against the Elderly

Most elderly persons are quite concerned about their personal investments because in most cases, those investments provide them with the majority, if not all, of their income. Since these investments are so important to their survival and quality of life, they need to be particularly cautious as to where they invest their money.

Scams and crimes against the elderly are not new; they have been going on for years. The poor eyesight and advanced age of the victims make them easy prey for criminals, and even if the crooks are caught, the sentences are usually light. One of my colleagues had an elderly grandmother who was ripped off in 1960 with an old scam still going on today. She was 85 years old and very sharp for her age. But she paid a complete stranger $250 to spray a revolutionary new product on her roof, a product that was guaranteed to stop leaks for 25 years. That new product was silver paint, and it washed off the roof during the first rain of the season.

What makes the elderly such easy targets? It is certainly not because they are foolish. I believe there are many factors. Today's generation of elderly grew up in a very different time. A handshake and a man's word were as good as money in the bank. This propensity for trust, combined with the possible separation from a spouse, a family that lives far away, and a slick con artist's empty promises, clouds their judgment.

The elderly are often lonely and desire someone, anyone, to talk to. The con men who prey on them have trained extensively to become proficient in scamming the elderly. They are professionals, if you will, at what they do. They can be very nice and attentive, or they can be threatening and intimidating, but the goal is always the same: Get the victim's money, as much of it as possible!

Remember our motto: Retention is always better than apprehension.

You are always better off not to lose your money in the first place than to expect the police to apprehend the crook and recover the money that the crook has already spent. Many of the scams and frauds already discussed throughout this book are used against the elderly; however, what follows are some of the more common fraud schemes being used today against senior citizens:

Ponzi Schemes

A Ponzi scheme is perpetrated when a suspect offers investments or provides interest or dividends to old investors by using money from new investors. They are essentially robbing Peter to pay Paul. Early investors in such schemes may actually realize gains. The last investors in lose all, or most, of their money.

One type of Ponzi scheme is promissory note fraud, which has become the primary type of securities fraud in many states across the country. These scams have taken at least $300 million from thousands of elderly Americans. Regulators in retiree-rich Florida have taken the lead in coordinating a 38-state task force to fight promissory note fraud. Florida-based scams have defrauded $100 million out of 1,000 victims, mostly senior citizens. This scam is currently Connecticut's No. 1 securities fraud as well, with victims losing more than $10 million.

Promissory Note Fraud

There are some retired people who invest their money by loaning it to lending institutions, who then provide the funds for homeowners who desire to take out a second mortgage on their home for home improvements, to consolidate credit card debts, or for whatever reasons. When these retired persons lend that money to the mortgage company, they expect to receive back interest on the money they have lent.

However, some investors fall prey to con artists working a second trust deed scam. The con artist supposedly gives interest to investors on second trust deeds on properties, when in fact, such deeds stand in fourth or fifth place. As you may recall from the real estate chapter, such deeds are made when people use the equity in their home as security for a second mortgage to obtain a loan. In this case there is a promissory note, with a second trust deed to back up that promissory note, and that is why this procedure is called taking out a second mortgage on their home. This trust deed now stands in second position behind the original note on the property. That is, the first (original) deed has legal priority to be paid off first in the event of foreclosure or sale of the property, and if there is any money left over, then the second note will be paid off.

A promissory note that stands in fourth or fifth position behind (subordinated to) other notes will usually be a worthless piece of paper, as there would not be enough equity in the property to pay off the earlier notes. The scam artist knows this, but uses the formal paperwork because it looks good as a sales tool and is technically legal even though it is worthless. He will peddle these notes as second notes even though he knows that they actually stand in fourth or fifth position. Perhaps the note buyers will even receive payments for a time on these notes, until the day the checks stop coming and the con man is nowhere to be found.

In a similar, yet more sophisticated arrangement, some promissory notes are a type of short-term debt companies use to borrow cash. The notes are almost always classified as securities, which must be registered with the state and sold by licensed securities brokers. However, con artists try to use a loophole in securities laws that exempts certain nine-month promissory notes from regulatory scrutiny.

Under the guise of a marketing company, the con artists seek out struggling start-up companies that need money. The marketing firms then recruit independent insurance agents around the country to sell the bogus notes, which typically come with a worthless repayment guarantee from a fake foreign insurance company. Foreign currencies are sometime involved as well, which is one hallmark of a bogus securities scam. The companies have been known to use the money from new notes to pay the interest on old notes, in classic Ponzi style, so investors often don't know anything is wrong until the notes are due and suddenly in default.

The scam has spread quickly because it sounds like a safe deal with a good return on one's investment. The notes typically pay a 9% to 12% annual rate and are promoted as risk free because they are supposedly insured. After nine months, investors are told, they will get their money back or have the option of rolling it over into a new nine-month note. These notes are sold by local insurance agents, who have sold their clients safe products for years, such as life insurance policies. The insurance agents, who are paid a nice commission by these companies, say that they themselves are often fooled by the notes.

In some similar scams the investors are told that they must maintain confidential information about the investment program. The promoter may even require that the investors sign a confidentiality agreement. In a legitimate investment deal, however, a potential investor should be able to contact past investors to find out more about their experiences. A potential investor should ask the promoter, "Have you had success with this investment in the past?" If the answer is no, seek another investment. If the answer is yes, contact and validate references, making sure that those references are legitimate sources.

Watch out for these red flags:

1. Any promissory notes of nine-month duration.

2. Notes promising a high rate of return of 9 to 18 percent.

3. Notes promising guaranteed investments.

4. Notes involving unusual foreign currencies or foreign banks or insurance companies. Always have your banker verify the validity of any offshore or out-of-country bank, the validity of the account, and the availability of funds.

5. Requests to sign confidentiality agreements.

Bogus Invoicing to Alzheimer's Patients

A new scheme just brought to my attention is perpetrated when a hospital worker gained access to a list of Alzheimer's patients, which included their billing addresses. This creative scammer used this list to mail bogus, but authentic-looking, invoices to these unsuspecting senior citizens, and many of them were paid. Seniors who are still paying their own bills need to check invoices against existing files to verify that they are paying for either a normal monthly bill or something they truly ordered.

Romance Scams

These are also known by many in law enforcement as "sweetheart scams." Unlike many other types of scams, most romance scams are run by solo mavericks. Often, particularly sleazy scam artists use the guise of romance to get their victims to divulge personal information about themselves or relinquish control of their assets. If romance has come to you too easily, then maybe something is wrong. Many elderly persons have been victimized by younger companions who have taken advantage of them.

A typical romance scam setup involves a younger woman romancing a man and then moving into his home. Now she is in a position to do any number of things. For example, she might convince him to add her name to his signature cards at the bank so that she can "help out" by paying the bills. Then she could either embezzle funds or simply clear out the bank accounts altogether.

Another trick she might try is to convince him to add her name to the title on his vehicles or properties. Now she can refinance the property and take the money and run, or worse yet, when the elderly man's health fails to the point of hospitalization, or if he dies, she can sell the property and disappear before the rightful heirs can remedy the problem.

Here is a disturbing case I recently worked. An elderly man was actually on his deathbed, with the doctors fully expecting the man's imminent demise. While he was in wrist restraints and on morphine, a renegade chaplain performed a brief confidential ceremony wedding him to a younger woman intent on a romance scam. The family has not been able to locate this minister, and their attorney had to issue a subpoena to the county recorder's office just to get a copy of the confidential marriage certificate. The woman obviously knew what she was doing and orchestrated the situation in her favor because, as the wife, she was able to acquire all of the man's property upon his demise.

But women are also swindled by men who feign love in exchange for monetary considerations. There was such a man who publicly boasted about bilking women out of large sums of money using a romance scam. He would talk his new-found lover into putting up $100,000 to supposedly match his $100,000 toward an investment. These women would simply write him a check. He would then stash the money away in his own secret account, but later he would explain that the investment had suffered a sudden and total loss. His lover was out the $100,000, but he now had the money in his possession to spend at his leisure. I think it's a bad idea to mix romance with business—anytime.

I do not give you this information to scare you, but to make you aware of what is happening in the world today. The following suggestions are offered to prepare you and protect you so that you won't be victimized by these scams. You must stay alert and know what is going on around you. Con men move around all over the country. If you are an easy mark one time, they will give your name to another con man, and before you know it, you are on a list of easy marks.

Also, keep in mind that your local police department is there to protect you. If you feel uncomfortable or frightened, or for any other reason feel you are about to be ripped off, call 911.

Checklist for the Elderly: Protecting Your Assets

1. If anyone approaches you or calls you and asks you any questions about your money or tries to get any financial information about you, immediately terminate the conversation. If the person becomes abusive or pushy, call 911.

2. If you need some type of work done on your house, yard, or car, never use someone going door to door. Rely on local contractors or mechanics. Check for references. Check with friends, neighbors, or relatives for referrals to competent, qualified contractors. Remember, qualified contractors who do good work do not have to go door to door for business!

3. Do not give out any personal information on the phone. Never give your credit card information to anyone that calls you! If you call a company to make a purchase on the phone, however, that's different.

4. Do not open your door or let strangers in your home for any reason. Speak to them through the door. If they have an emergency, offer to make a call for them. Remember, if you open your door to a stranger, you may become the victim of a home invasion robbery.

5. Have your checking account set up so that two signatures are required for checks in excess of the amount you normally would write. If you don't have a relative or friend you can rely on, simply have your checks printed with a second signature line. Then you can always tell anyone who tries to get you to write a large check that it takes a second signature.

6. When paying bills, check invoices against existing files to verify that you are paying for either a normal monthly bill or something that you truly ordered.

7. Do not keep large amounts of cash on your person or hidden in your home. This type of information spreads like wildfire, and you may become the victim of a home invasion robbery.

8. There are no law enforcement agencies or bank examiners that use your money for any type of investigation. If someone tries to engage you in this type of scheme, call the police.

9. Before investing in a promissory note on a specific property, call your local title insurance company and have them run a Preliminary Title Inspection Report. This report is usually free and will show how many notes are against the property and what the property is worth. If you are new to these investments, have a trusted broker or at least a knowledgeable friend take you through the process.

10. When investing in portfolios of numerous promissory notes, avoid investments that require secrecy and/or request that you sign a confidentiality agreement. You should consider these requests to be red flags of bogus investments.

CHAPTER FOURTEEN

COMPUTER AND INTERNET FRAUD

Outsmarting High-Tech Scammers

all me old-fashioned, but despite my enthusiasm for today's technology, I still like to pick up a pen and actually write just to
remember what it feels like. There is something satisfying and
reminiscent about taking pen in hand and feeling it scratch and roll against
the paper fibers, watching as my thoughts transfer to the written page
through my hand.

I'm not stuck in the past, though: I also use computers all day long,
and my typing speed was clocked at 113 words per minute when I used
to do data entry work. I was also writing computer programs in the Basic
and Fortran languages in 1969. It has been quite interesting to watch
computers develop from the industrial IBM 360 model 40s, to the home
model TRS-80s, to XTs and the ATs in the mid 80s, and so on through
what we have today. When I bought an XT in 1984, it had 20 megabytes
of storage. I remember thinking then, "What in the world will anybody
ever do with twenty megabytes?" Now that we measure hard drives in
gigabytes, I wonder, What will be the standard fifteen years hence?

I still work cases today that revolve around documents prepared and
signed ten, twenty, and even fifty years ago. Any document that you have
ever signed or been connected to in the past can come under dispute
today or tomorrow and go to arbitration or court litigation. Similarly, all
the documents that you and others are preparing today are important
now, but will also carry significance into the future.

The trend today is toward documents being transferred, read, and archived via computers, with this information never ending up being printed to paper. I think there will come a day when writing instruments become obsolete, and future generations will have a glazed look of confusion when the "paper" of commerce is discussed. They will wonder why past generations ever bothered with such crude and archaic nuisances. But that day has not yet come. I personally believe that hard documents, that is, paper documents, are still going to be with us for the next thirty years, only in decreasing numbers.

As we are now implementing new applications for computer technology and e-commerce every day, along with these new technologies come new methods of forging, counterfeiting, and committing fraud by creative "e-criminals." Let's see what e-criminals are doing today and learn how to guard against their strikes.

"Desktop Counterfeiting"

Although already being used effectively, desktop counterfeiting is continually perfecting itself with every newer generation of printer that comes on the market. Printer technology is just now catching up to the imaging programs that offer excellent quality and tools for creating counterfeit instruments. Since most bank checks and other negotiable instruments have such varied designs and because today's computer printers perform so well, counterfeit checks can be difficult to spot. Counterfeiting checks is an inexpensive way to steal millions with just a small amount of skill. Bad checks can easily be cashed in supermarkets and department stores because cashiers often have little training in recognizing them.

The way to keep your business from being victimized by these counterfeiters is to acquaint all cashiers or money-handlers with the appearance of computer color-printed materials. With training, they will be able to spot an ink-jet printed check. Why not have your home or office computer whiz play the game of trying to make the best-possible ink-jet copy of a few of your canceled checks? Then let your clerks make their own comparisons. Remember, however, that some consumers may create their own legitimate checks using their home computers and printers. Therefore, if you determine that a check was printed on a home ink-jet printer, that does not necessarily mean that the check is bogus. Review Chapter 6 for other methods of recognizing counterfeit checks.

Pharmacy employees must also be on the lookout for forged

prescriptions. The simplest form of this kind of fraud involves photo-copying a legitimate prescription after whiting out the original informa-tion, then forging the fresh copy. More elaborate techniques involve us-ing a computer scanner, then reprinting the prescription on a laser printer or an ink-jet printer. Thirty minutes of training for employees should be sufficient to learn to recognize the differences between offset lithographic printing methods and xerographic and ink-jet printing technologies. I advise doctors to continue using prescription forms that are offset-pro-duced and to advise the local drug stores that this is their custom. This will offer local pharmacies a quick way to identify counterfeited prescrip-tion forms.

The counterfeiting of stock certificates and identity documents is on the increase as scanners and computer printers are catching up with the image quality offered by traditional print-shop methods of offset lithog-raphy. Questioned Document Experts will still be able to tell whether the printing method used to create such documents was lithographic, xero-graphic, or ink-jet technology, which will ultimately determine the valid-ity of such stock certificates and identity documents. Remember, though, that the purpose of the counterfeiter is not to fool the documents expert, but only to fool the victim at the point of transfer, who will take that certificate in trade for something of value or accept the bogus identity document to back up a worthless check. Greater scrutiny of such nego-tiable items and identity documents is more important now than ever.

Another trend I have observed is that the "fancy" papers are not be-ing used so much any more. Law firms and corporations are no longer electing to use "laid paper" or papers with watermarks. Everybody seems to be going to generic bond papers, which eliminates one of the basic avenues of investigation in the arena of questioned document examina-tion. The use of such generic paper makes it easier for the counterfeiters to find a paper that is similar to the paper they want to imitate in the preparation of the bogus contract, will, or deed. Thus, using a more readily-distinguishable paper can make your unique documents more difficult to counterfeit.

Cut-and-Paste Forgeries

This could also be called "desktop forgery" since it is just another application of the basic desktop counterfeiting techniques, only applied to signatures. Indeed, the cut-and-paste forgeries discussed in Chapter 3 continue to grow in frequency. Whereas five years ago I saw these cases only occasionally, I now seem them regularly. Document examiners can tell if signatures have been created as the result of "cut-and-paste" technologies, but that discussion is too lengthy for our purposes here. Just be sure to keep copies of documents that you sign for as long as it is practical.

Digitized Authorizing Signatures

I just purchased four shirts at a local Macy's, and to authorize the purchase I had to sign on a capture pad using a stylus. Of course, the purpose of this capture device is to store the signature in a database for later reference. It does not authenticate your signature. After signing, I noticed that the image of my signature was very poor, and it also didn't look much like my normal signature due to the limited writing area, the unnatural movement of the stylus on the writing pad, and the poor dpi (dots per inch resolution) of the software used. I walked away thinking that it would be very easy for me to later call and deny that I had actually made that transaction since the signature did not appear to be my normal true signature. This, in fact, is what many people do, and this scam usually works.

Despite the limitations of these digitized signature pads, large national chains seem to be moving toward making them their only instrument of verification of a transaction by a card holder. Such devices are also being used to "confirm" receipts of deliveries of parcels. The problem with this kind of system is that there is no original copy of a signature that shows pen speed and pressure, pen direction, and other details so important to authenticate a signature or conversely, to demonstrate forgery. I have been provided printed copies of such receipts in casework, but these documents are very difficult to deal with. They are often of little value in proving that somebody did or did not sign a receipt.

In my view, companies wishing to use this technology should invest in products that yield higher dpi, as well as provide a larger writing area on the tablet and a writing surface that offers more resistance (drag), such as we feel on a document when we write on paper. Otherwise, companies should stick with paper and receipts, or take a thumbprint (see Chapters 6 and 11 on the "inkless fingerprint program"). New technology is not only supposed to make things faster and easier; it is also supposed to make things better. In my experience, some "new technologies" are a step backward in methods of authentication.

Computer Date/Time Changes

Most people know how to change a computer's internal clock using Windows or some other operating program, but there are other more sophisticated ways to do so.

Just as it is important to keep copies of paper documents, it is also important to keep copies of computer file contracts and other important documents that pertain to you and your business dealings. The same basic reasons apply, and you will now see why. Computer files can be backdated or postdated by simple alteration of the internal clock.

Imagine that you and I entered into a contract that was dated September 15, 1997, but you never received a hard copy of that contract. A dispute has arisen between us concerning this contract now. It would be in my best interest during litigation if the contract were dated a year before we actually entered into our agreement. I could get into my computer today, change the clock, then recreate the file, typing the earlier date "September 15, 1996," and also saving the file on that same backdated day. After doing this, I could then reset the computer's clock to the proper date, and nobody would be able to prove what I had done, at least not without a forensic hard-drive analysis.

If you and I then went to arbitration or court, I could produce the actual computer file with its fraudulent date/time stamp, showing the court my version of the date of our contractual agreement. This evidence could be convincing to the court, particularly if you came to court with no evidence on your behalf and with no evidence to prove my case wrong. Backdated and post-dated documents will continue to be deciphered by locating the computer file on backed-up "mirror-image" tapes that produced them, then looking up the file date and time stamp under "Properties" or by other means using computer utility programs. The following steps can help prevent time/date stamp scams:

1. Notarize important paper agreements, and keep copies, if not the originals.

2. Also obtain a copy of the computer file that generated the document. Have the person who prepared the file (if it was not you) e-mail you a copy of the file. Make sure that the file's date corresponds to the appropriate time period, then save it to a floppy disk. You should also include that file as

part of a mirror-image backup tape (see below) since this procedure will place the file date of the document under consideration with other files backed up at that same time. Put that disk in the file folder that contains your hard copy and the other documents concerning this agreement, and note the location of the back-up tape.

3. Do regular mirror-image backups (see below), which will provide you a record of all contracts and other documents you have prepared on your end.

4. Review and implement the suggestions for preparing iron-clad contracts in Chapter 4.

Saving and Deleting of Computer Files

Can an employee really cover his tracks after ravaging the corporate computers?

In most cases, there's really no such thing as "deleted data." It's still there in pieces, resting on your hard drive. For instance, if you write a letter, perhaps using Microsoft Word, you might save it as "letter.doc." When you tell the computer to save your letter, the read-write head looks for blank spaces on the disk, then fills them with the contents of your letter. The computer knows where these blank spaces are because it keeps a list of them in a special file called the File Allocation Table ("FAT").

Obviously, we wouldn't want to keep a list of every tiny blank spot on the disk big enough for one period or comma of your letter. Instead the computer keeps a list of larger blank areas, called clusters, that can each contain hundreds of sentences. Our disk's clusters are made big enough that there won't be too long a list of them for the computer to remember in the FAT. As a consequence, some clusters can contain a great deal of data.

When you delete a file, the computer does it the easy way: instead of scrubbing the data from the clusters one by one, it just puts the clusters back on the list of empty ones in the FAT. Until you save another file, the content of your letter is still on the hard disk—it's not overwritten until you try to save another file to the hard disk, and the system writes new data into these clusters that have now been labeled as empty. What's more, if your old letter was a full cluster long, and the new file is only half a cluster long, the second half of your original letter still remains. Because the cluster is now listed as occupied by, say, "letter2.doc," that second half is protected from erasure or deletion. This means that data, or evidence of wrongdoing, can linger on a computer hard drive for a very long time.

So we've seen how persistent the data on a hard drive can be. This means that if you believe one of your company computers or laptops may at one time have contained important evidence, you may be able to retrieve that evidence by contacting a data forensics expert or hard-disk analyst. This person would use your backup archives to investigate any possible computer fraud that has occurred either on your server or on one of your company's workstations. Now you see the importance of saving computer information!

"Data" and "Mirror-Image" Backups

Even if you have a small business with only one computer, you should still do regular backups, as well as considering the following advice for medium to larger companies. Just as I advise maintaining records of hard copies of documents, you should also keep copies of computer files you generate. With that in mind, you should be archiving your files for storage so that you will have your own record that you can produce as proof against someone who has, for example, brought a document's date into question by post-dating your computer file. The person who does produce records in any litigation, even if they are phony, will most likely win the case if the other side has no evidence to offer. So let's talk about what types of backups you should do and how often you should do them.

There are two kinds of backups you should consider—"data" and "mirror-image" backups. These could also be expressed as "archival" and "forensic" backups. Data backups just copy the visible files; mirror-image backups copy every bit of every cluster (including that letter you thought you'd overwritten in the example given above).

First there are the useful data backups of simple day-to-day information, such as numerous letters, contracts, or data images that need to be kept together. If you are a smaller company with only one or two computers, to do a data backup you need to purchase a data storage device. There are many devices available that take advantage of a number of media. For smaller companies you might find it sufficient to perform data backups using a CD writer. If you don't already have one, your local computer store can install one onto your existing computer. Try to find one that best suits your needs. Larger companies with servers and workstations also perform data backups nightly, as well as performing "system backups" weekly.

But if your company is large enough to have a network system—and when it comes to performing backups for fraud prevention—you should make regular mirror-image backups to tape on perhaps a monthly basis. The timing and type of backups you keep should be based on your unique business model. A qualified data security specialist can study your individual situation and tailor the appropriate backup procedures.

You should consider storing selected old backup tapes instead of re-using them. You'll have to spend more money on tapes and store more of them, but you'll also have an indelible record of all of the computer files on each backed-up server or machine as of the date of each backup. Backup tapes are more difficult to alter than the contents of the original computer hard drive. From a fraud prevention standpoint, they are the best way to go.

If someone re-dates crucial correspondence or alters bookkeeping entries, the backup will reveal it. Should someone claim he was never exposed to certain secret company information, the forensic-type backup can prove otherwise. It can prove this even if the material was on his system for only a short time before he deleted it. Bear in mind, however, that the longer a computer is used after suspect material has been deleted, the greater the risk the deleted material may be unrecoverable.

Back up your data or inventory control system every night on the server. Make sure that all of the employees know it is company policy that they must store their data on the server. You should also consider removing all floppy drives from computer workstations so that important company information cannot be saved to disk and removed from the business premises. Make it company policy that no personal files are to be stored on individual computers.

And here is an important final note in all of this: chances are that your Information Technology ("IT") employees know more than you ever will about your computers and your network system. It is imperative that you be able to totally trust these people because they control all of the company's information, which in turn is your lifeblood. The following discussion will reinforce why it is so important to have trusted and skilled IT people at the helm of your company's computer system.

Fraud in Network Environments

"Hacker" is a term of respect used in reference to skilled computer technicians who know how to get in, over, around, and through computer networks. But as in all things, there is also the dark side of the hacker, the one who uses his skills to destroy and steal. The following discussion offers advice to prevent successful attacks from these disreputable computer hackers. Your trained and experienced IT person is your best defense against hackers.

Why might someone want to hack into your computer?

1. To obtain personal data, such as credit card numbers, bank accounts, etc.

2. To obtain your account password or company data.

3. To commit corporate espionage.

4. To slow or stop the flow of business.

5. To obtain any programs you may have installed on your computer.

6. To falsify data that is residing on your computer.

7. Just for the bragging rights!

There are several ways that a hacker attacks. He can dig through your trash dumpster and find anything useful. He can find weaknesses in your network and then enter it from a remote location. He can even find the servers, at which point a hacker can do many things. He can find your master password list and then copy it to his computer, where he will run a cracking utility to decode the information on the file. Once he does this, he will have all of the user names, groups, passwords, and access rights for all of the users.

A hacker can cause your computer system to crash by flooding the server with packets of data or with processor commands. This will open a program in the server that just keeps getting bigger until the computer can't handle it and crashes. Or he can go after one of the client systems, where he can obtain data, monitor keystrokes, and create pinpoint problems in the network specifically in conjunction with his objectives.

If a hacker is working with your competitor, he may time his attacks with your competitor's business moves. Or the hacker could be a disgruntled employee—or a bitter former employee. To help protect your computers from hackers, we first need to establish a golden rule of security. If you are connected to a network, other computers can connect to you! Therefore, you must build your security to be strong inside as well as out.

Your computer transmits and receives data through "ports" that act like highways, allowing data to be simultaneously sent and received. Your computer has thousands of ports. Most are left open if you use a Windows 95 or 98 operating system. If you are using NT, Unix, or Linux, you can set up a far better security system by closing certain ports and allowing data to be sent or received only through a few ports that you specify. All of the ports may or may not be open on your system, but any open port is a hole in your defenses. You can also set up port monitoring and fake ports that are monitored, effectively creating a booby trap to catch a hacker.

Preventing External Attacks

Have a "firewall" in front of your computer to deter outside attacks. A firewall is like a gate: you can allow or block access by certain users and specify which "pathways" (ports) may or may not be used. The ports are the pathways through which that access travels. This is a big step to keep your company secrets and information safe from outside intruders.

If you have two divisions in your company, managers with security information and general employees, your IT employee can place firewalls to keep certain groups from having access to certain portions of the computer, for example, the accounting information. You also need to place a firewall between your Internet provider and your business computer system. This will control what information is allowed in from or out to your Internet provider.

Run virus protection software regularly. Even though I am usually very careful about using my software, in a few instances of hurry, I allowed 31 new Melissa viruses to sneak into my computer. I noticed my computer was behaving a bit mysteriously, so I ran my virus protection and sure enough, it caught and repaired these viruses. This was a good reminder to me to leave the virus auto-protect feature on when connected to the Internet.

Prior to this occurrence, one day in 1999, two out of three of my computers just went blank when I turned them on. That was the result of the first onslaught of the Melissa virus that struck hundreds of thousands of people. This cost me lots of important information, as well as at least fifty hours of my time restoring computers to the conditions they were in before the strike.

Many people who have come to rely on the "pocket pals" computer organizers lost all of their data—personal and business phone contacts as well as calendar information—when these machines fell prey to a virus. Remember to back up data, but also remember to diversify, even in the little things. That means having paper back-up systems, such as that "outdated" daily planner that fits in your back pocket or purse.

These vicious viruses are really a form of espionage. They not only destroy important information, but they also interrupt commerce. Make sure you have invested in good anti-virus software, and run your scanning and updating programs regularly. Always leave on your virus program auto-protect feature.

Close the retired equipment loophole. Because data can linger for a long time on computer hard drives, you should never sell company computer equipment without first removing the old hard drives and installing new ones. Consider that once something is written to a hard drive, it can be there forever.

Sophisticated government labs can even recover data from parts of clusters which have been scrubbed with commercial software utilities and filled with new data (or, in our example above, those parts of "letter.doc" that have been overwritten by "letter2.doc" in the first half of the cluster). It is not unnecessary caution that has inspired the U.S. government to decree that the only permissible method of clearing classified information from a hard drive requires both physical mutilation and incineration. (Then, they say, stir the ashes.)

Checklist: Tightening Up Your Network Security

1. Guard what ends up in the trash; remember to shred paper documents.

2. Change your passwords monthly or bimonthly.

3. Give all employees (especially managers) passwords that don't

mean anything. They should be at least seven characters long, containing 1-2 symbols and a good mix of letters and numbers.

4. If anyone gets fired, change all access rights and VPN (virtual private networking) logons immediately.

5. Ensure that internal security is just as tight as external security.

6. Close all ports that do not need to be open.

7. Include firewalls in your system.

8. Run virus protection software.

9. Destroy old hard-drives before disposing of them.

10. Ensure the happiness and loyalty of your IT employees. Give them a good annual bonus!

Using Internet Technologies to Commit Fraud

By the end of the year 2000, it is estimated that ten trillion transactions will have taken place on the Internet. It must be understood that the Internet is not just your computer browser; it is the connection of all computers. Some people think that the Internet consists of only Web pages. But there is so much more that goes on behind those simple icons and text that you see.

When you turn on your computer and surf the Internet, the pictures you see are in the result of html codes. "Html" stands for HyperText Markup Language and may also be expressed as "htm." This has been the type of programming language used to create and organize the text and images that you see on web pages. They are transferred from computer to computer via the http method, that is, "hyper text transfer protocol." Http is only one language of many used by computers to transfer data on the Internet.

The predecessors to http were ftp (file transfer protocol) and ntp (newsgroups), but these were not-user friendly and therefore not used by the masses, but only by computer technicians. The easily-navigated point-and-click method (http) of moving around from webpage to webpage marked the beginning of popular use of the Internet. But behind the friendly, innocent appearance of http are all these other languages that can still be used by hackers to gain access to wherever they want to go.

Forty years ago, people reacted against allowing the government and corporate America to know too much about their personal affairs and store such personal information for various uses. Back then such a concept was referred to as "Big Brother." Today it is "Big Browser" or the Internet, that has become the peeper and reaper of personal information. Identity thieves can steal customers' personal information from the Internet and use it for fraudulent purposes. Similarly, such information can be stolen from other sources and then used on the Internet to steal money or to commit other frauds or crimes against persons. Web sites, chat rooms, bulletin boards, and e-mailing are new tools used by scammers to supplement their old methods of using the phone, the U.S. mail, or door-to-door canvassing to contact their potential victims.

Online auction sales remained the number one Internet fraud for 1999, followed by sales of general merchandise, Internet access services, and work-at-home plans. With these concerns in mind, great care should be exercised when you come across these offers while browsing through cyberspace.

Auction Fraud on the Internet

In late June, a Yahoo user who identified himself as "harddrives4sale" began auctioning off four hard drives every day for about two weeks. He urged auction winners to use the PayPal service (which allows buyers to deposit funds for auction purchases), claiming he would get his money sooner and thus could deliver the hard drivers sooner. At least fifty people sent the money via PayPal, but no one received any of the hard drives. Since there is no mechanism to stop payment or contest charges against their PayPal accounts, the victims have no prospects for getting their money back.

Many online auction sites simply list items that people want to sell without verifying if the merchandise actually exists or is properly represented. It is up to the buyer to validate the item and the reliability of the seller. To verify company information, buyers should contact the state or local consumer protection agency and Better Business Bureau where the company is located. In addition, look at the auction site's feedback section for comments about the seller. Be aware that glowing reports could be "planted" by the seller, and that a clean complaint record does not guarantee that a seller is legitimate.

Be especially careful if the seller is a private individual. Most consumer protection laws and the government agencies that enforce them don't deal with private sales, so if you have a problem, you won't have any legal recourse. Get the seller's name, street address, and telephone number to check him or her out or to follow up if there is a problem. Don't do business with sellers who won't provide such information. Ask about policies for delivery, returns, warranties, and service. Agree on a definite delivery time, and request that the shipment be insured. Pay by credit card because you can dispute the charges if the goods are misrepresented or never arrive. File a complaint with the auction site if you have a problem with a buyer or purchase.

Be extremely cautious when purchasing collectibles. The collectibles market is riddled with fraud to begin with, so even under the best of circumstances, you have a greater chance of purchasing a fake item than the real McCoy. Since you can't examine the item or have it appraised until after the sale, you can't assume that claims made about it are valid. I advise against buying collectibles on the Internet. If you do, however, insist on getting a written statement describing the item and its value before you pay. If possible, have someone you know who lives near the seller go and check out the item for you.

Checklist: Internet Auction Purchases

1. Be careful to whom you give your financial or other personal information.
2. Take your time to decide, and be mindful that high-pressure sales tactics are often signs of fraud.
3. Be aware that there are differences between sales by private individuals and sales by businesses. You typically have stronger legal rights when dealing with a business rather than an individual.
4. Recognize that unsolicited e-mailings are often used by con artists.

Credit Card Fraud on the Internet

Credit card fraud occurs not just in brick-and-mortar stores, but also over the Internet. In fact, VISA recently reported that online fraud is running at more than three times the rate of regular credit card fraud overall. They predict that the volume of online purchases will quintuple by 2003, and with these added transactions comes the threat of additional fraud.

Unsuspecting America Online members have recently been lured into giving up credit card information over the Internet by two 15-year-old hackers. The teens used the credit card numbers to buy thousands of dollars' worth of online goods. The two allegedly sent subscribers phony e-mails with AOL chief executive Steve Case's name, asking them to go to a Web site to update subscriber information, including credit card data.

A different group of hackers constructed a web site that posed as an "anti-fraud" web site of the American Association of Retired Persons (AARP). The site requested that members update their credit information. The hackers were able to place charges against the credit cards of members who signed up for this "monthly service."

Before using your credit card on the Internet, be sure to look at the address screen—that is, that information after the http://www. in your browser's window—to make sure that you have gone to the web page you intended to access. It is very easy to make a mistake and inadvertently end up at a dangerous web site.

Purchasing Software on the Internet

Making software purchases on the Internet from second hand ("after market") sources is risky unless you are quite sure about the seller's reputation. It is common for software counterfeiters to sell products such as Microsoft Office that are copies of original disks, only with a little surprise: a Trojan horse program inside. When you install the program onto your computer, it will work fine—but you may also be installing a hacking program that will allow the hacker to gain access to your entire computer database. After he is done collecting whatever data he was after, the program may or may not crash your system.

Instead of purchasing such discounted software over the Internet, you may be better off paying the higher retail price to avoid potential losses from computer crashes or system failures. One word of warning: if the price is too good to be true, then the item is probably counterfeit.

Another way for hackers to access your computer system is through a web site called "napster" or "rapster," which allows users to download free music. The problem is that while your system is connected to these sites, these other sites are also connected to your computer system. People may be browsing your hard drive to steal programs or discrete company information—or to crash your system. Consider the potential hazards of such sites before allowing your employees to browse them on company computers.

Prescription Drug Sales on the Internet

Recently, four people were charged with conspiring to illegally sell prescription drugs over the Internet. The defendants used a computer to create phony prescriptions that bore the name of a foreign doctor. Assistant Attorney General David Ogden warned, "Internet sites that claim to provide the services of a doctor when a prescription is issued on the basis of answers to questions on a form can be scams." Various government agencies continue to monitor such activities.

Espionage and the Internet

In a report out of London, researchers at Notre Dame University are concerned that "cyber-terrorists" could take advantage of key nodes that allow information to travel on the Internet. The team says if cyber-terrorists learned how to disrupt these nodes, the World Wide Web could essentially be fragmented into isolated parts and virtually shut down. We should all exercise caution in our businesses and remember the old adage, "Don't put all of your eggs in one basket." When it comes to commerce, including advertising, we should rely on various media so that when there is a temporary interruption in one medium, we may fall back on others.

Bulletin Board Fraud on the Internet

Web page bulletin boards are another place where scammers set up their snares. Most commercial bulletin-board services allow individuals to post messages under one or more aliases. Since it may be impossible for another subscriber to determine the true identity of the individual behind the message, there is enormous potential for fraud. One type of fraud perpetrated on bulletin boards is manipulation of the stock of little-known companies that have a small float (the number of shares available to be bought and sold).

Acting alone or with accomplices, one company insider, broker, public relations executive, or even just a large shareholder can leave numerous messages calculated to spark interest in an obscure stock. Once a "thread" (in this case, a series of related messages about a stock) is started, it will show up on the computer bulletin board and be readily accessible by anyone who enters the bulletin board. As interest builds, dozens of messages may be posted about the stock, such as the following examples of a typical bulletin-board scam:

> *"Is anyone out there following Company X?"*

> *"I heard that Company X is about to make a major announcement. E-mail me or call this toll-free number to get an information package."*

> *"I spoke to Company X's CEO, who confirmed details of next month's big news. I've bought 10,000 shares. Look for share price to double in next month! Get it now!"*

> *"Big news is just around the corner. We hear from a friend who has visited Company X that it's going to be even bigger than we thought. There's still time to get in."*

> *"Short sellers are in the market! Keep the faith... This will bounce back. The smart money will use the price as an opportunity to buy more and dollar average."*

Through a combination of puffery, speculation, and breathless claims of supposedly inside information about pending announcements, product innovations, and new contracts, the schemers seek to run up the price of the stock, which starts rising as unwary investors read of the "great opportunity" and buy shares. In response, the insiders take their shares (bought at the low, "pre-hype" prices) and sell them into the rising market.

When the hype-fueled stock price falters, the promoters may blame unnamed short sellers. A "short seller" is a person who sells a stock short, which is in essence, structuring the sell/purchase arrangement of the stock such that the buyer anticipates that the stock will lose rather than gain value. Sometimes, losses suffered by the unsuspecting are made even worse by ruthless promoters who urge victims to "dollar average" and keep buying shares, even at the falling prices. Talk of the stock then disappears from the board. Investors who are left holding the bag can do little more than post plaintive messages: "Whatever happened to Company X?"

Online Work-At-Home Offers

Don't believe promises that you can make a small fortune easily by working at home. If that were true, we'd all be doing it! Get all the details in writing before you pay for anything. You may find that the work is very different from the description that was e-mailed to you. It is not customary that you would pay first to get this information. Work-at-home plans for envelope stuffing, for example, are classic illegal pyramid schemes in which victims are instructed to lure other people into paying to find out how to make money. These "workers" end up mailing the same information they received to other potential workers. These scams are often presented as legal and may even mention a federal law, but they may actually violate that law.

Do your homework before accepting any work-at-home offer. Find out if there is a market for the work you would be doing. If the promoter claims to have customers for this work, ask for their contact information and confirm the promoter's claim directly. If the work will be for professionals, such as invoicing for doctors, contact several in your area to find out if they actually employ people to work for them from home. Be aware of legal requirements as well. To do some types of work, such as medical billing, you may need a license or a certificate. Check with your state attorney general's office.

You should also ask for references of other people who have been doing the work, then contact them directly to ensure the validity of the program. Get the refund, buy-back, and cancellation policies in advance— and in writing. Be leery of seminars that promise to help you make money. These are often high-pressure sales pitches for overpriced motivational materials, unusable software, or information that is generally available for free at the library.

These are just some of the scams on the Internet today. More appear every day. If you believe that you have been victimized by some type of Internet fraud scheme, there is a central clearing house where you can lodge a complaint. It is the Internet Fraud Complaint Center, or IFCC. This is a partnership between the FBI and the National White Collar Crime Center. You can visit their web site at http://www.ifccfbi.gov/.

E-mail

Every electronic-mail message, or e-mail, is similar to regular U.S. mail you send through your local post office in that it has a destination address, a return address, and of course, a message. The return address for e-mail is not something that the sender puts on it; instead it is automatically generated by the computer, along with a time and date stamp. Your Internet Service Provider ("ISP") acts like the "mailman," delivering your message to the addressee.

E-mail Abuses

E-mail can be abused in several ways, one of which is e-mail spoofing. This occurs when someone sends a message but changes the header information (the sender's information) so that the message appears to be coming from somebody else. Some types of e-mail on which this spoofing technique is used are annoying advertisements, threatening and/or harassing messages, and pornographic image files. Anonymous writings may also be sent using the e-mail account of a different person so as to appear to be sent by that person. In other words, an innocent person can be "set up" to appear as the bad guy who is sending the harassing and abusive e-mail messages. This is a good argument to ensure that entry into your e-mail must be gained via password. Although it is convenient to set up your preferences so that you do not have to always input your password, I advise against doing so.

In addition to these misuses, a different e-mail abuse comes in the form of fictitious e-mail senders. It is very easy today to set up an account at places such as "Hotmail.com." A person can give fictitious information to establish a simple account, then use that account to harass others. The person can easily remain anonymous using this method, and you will not even begin to get a trace on this person without filing a criminal complaint, initiating an investigation which could only move ahead on the basis of search warrants.

A final e-mail problem is the silly chain e-mails that demand money be sent to a certain address or the person will be cursed. Although I'm sure that few people fall for this one, there are the chain e-mails started by a scammer writing a phony e-mail message about a friend that is dying from cancer. The message requests that money be sent to a certain address and that the original e-mail message be forwarded to ten other people. Many of these types of messages have been going around the country. Watch out for them.

One cannot predict how many additional ways e-mail will be abused in the future, so do yourself a favor now and implement these precautions. (Note: These do not apply to your Internet Service Provider.)

1. Be cautious about giving out your e-mail address, which can be used to access a lot of information about you.

2. When you set up an e-mail account, don't give your business or home address, your phone number, or your social security number.

3. Keep sensitive information out of your e-mails unless you use an encryption program, which prevents anyone from stealing your trade secrets or finding out with whom you are doing business.

E-Signatures

Digital signatures are also known as "e-signatures." An "e-document," such as an e-mail or a legal document, can be signed by use of a digital signature. The "private key" that guards these digital signatures is a computer code that only the sender knows... supposedly. But admittedly, if your private key is stolen, your signature can be fraudulently used by "e-forgers." I would avoid the use of digital signatures for the time being until the technology becomes more reliable. Please understand that although e-signature technology may be effective, its vulnerability to "e-bandits" has yet to be determined. I believe these e-criminals are wringing their hands in excitement over e-signatures and even now are devising their methods for fraud.

With the passage of recent legislation, electronic signatures on electronic contracts now have the same legal status as handwritten signatures on paper. The digital signature bill was cleared by the House of Representatives by a 426-4 vote on June 14, 2000, and was passed by the Senate on June 16, 2000 by an 87-0 margin. On June 30, 2000, President Clinton signed into law the Electronic Signatures in Global and National Commerce Act. Now, mortgages, loans and some other contracts may be signed using digital signatures. In his enthusiasm, President Clinton stated, "Customers will soon enjoy a whole new universe of online services..." My response is, "So will the e-fraudsters."

This bill leaves up for grabs how these new technologies will be implemented. Keep in mind that digital signatures are only as secure as the computers on which they are used. Many computers are not as secure as we would like to believe. Look at the Melissa virus, the "I love u virus," and other viruses that have been crashing computers all over the world recently.

There are a lot of ways that digital signatures can be stolen. None of them has to do with cracking the signature's code, that is, the code of the smart card. If private "keys" for digital signatures are stored on hard drives, then viruses can collect them and send them to e-criminals. Further, if a smart card reader connects to a virus-infested computer, the virus might hijack it. Let's wait and let these new technologies prove themselves before entrusting our important signatures to cyberspace.

Checklist: Preventing Internet Fraud

1. Buy software from reliable sources.

2. Think twice before allowing your employees to use company computers to browse on napster or rapster.

3. Do not ever give out your credit card information, social security, number, or other personal information to unsolicited contacts.

4. When making purchases online, look in the browser window at the address that begins with "http://www..." and make sure you know where you are!

5. Be very careful about the information you obtain from bulletin boards; it may be completely bogus.

6. Do not believe promises of making big bucks from Work-At-Home programs.

7. When communicating with strangers on the Internet, keep in mind that people may not be representing themselves in a truthful manner.

8. It may be smart to avoid the use of e-signatures for the time being until these technologies become more reliable.

DEALING WITH
ANONYMOUS DOCUMENTS

Investigating Espionage, Threats, and Harassment
in the Work Place

W hen I was first taking flying lessons at the Sacramento Executive Airport, I saw an unusual advertisement pinned to a bulletin board. It advertised a free pilot's license offered by a nearby flying club. The ad portrayed another club as the "No frills flying club," calling it the "Rent-A-Wreck" of general aviation. It claimed that the aero club cut corners in several ways. First the ad stated that the airplanes they used were antiques and that they obtained their replacement parts from irreputable sources. It also cited alleged incidents of electrical system failures, engine failures, gas tank fires, loss of landing gear, propellers flying off—all leading to "Actual In-flight Emergencies!"

None of this was true. Some time later I happened to be contacted by that aero club about these libelous posters, which I learned had been distributed all over area airports. I was informed that a present member of the club had had disagreements with the club officials and had been expressing himself in bizarre ways. He was suspected of shooting an actual bear cub and throwing it over the aero club's small airplane, called a "J-3 Cub." He had also stolen the club's computer, vandalized their offices, and stolen a plane, leaving it at a distant airfield with broken computer parts from the office strewn around on the ground.

This libelous ad was not handwritten nor typed by a typewriter. It was made with rub-on lettering and then photocopied. To the naked eye, there was not much that could be seen on the ad that might suggest any tie to anybody. However, one day one of the club owners noticed some small marks on the copy of this ad and wondered if anything could be done with them. These marks on the paper were extraneous toner marks, or "trash marks," put there inadvertently by a photocopy machine (see Chapter 2).

When the aero club officials contacted me about this, I informed them that it could be possible to make a tie with other documents, but we would need to come up with documents that could be associated with the suspect. One night, an investigator did a "garbage run" and found handfuls of documents thrown out in the suspect's garbage, then brought them to me for analysis. These documents were just copies of an invitation to a party that the suspect was going to have. When I examined them, however, I noticed that the exact same extraneous toner markings were on the invitation and the libelous ad. I was able to photograph these marks and create an exhibit to present to the aero club's board of directors, helping them make a decision to expel this member from the club.

Anonymous Notes and Letters

Every day in businesses around the country, company officials and employees receive anonymous notes and letters that are left on desks, inboxes, lockers, and car windows. Some of these notes may constitute sexual harassment if they are notes of lust or letters from spurned individuals angry over unreturned romantic or sexual advances. Some notes might be motivated by ethnic hatred. Some might simply be written by an employee who is angry at a coworker or at management. Indeed, some writings may threaten physical harm, death, espionage, or blackmail. Approximately once a month I'm contacted by an individual who requests that I, as a document examiner, determine which employee wrote an anonymous note. How should company owners, human resources managers, and executives respond to this common problem?

First, an anonymous note should be handled carefully. If you receive such a note, you should avoid having anyone else touch either the note itself or the envelope, if any, in which it was received. This will protect the document for a fingerprint examination if necessary. Also, writing ink can be damaged by excessive handling. If handwriting examinations are necessary, they will be most productive if the paper and ink have not been damaged by handling. Such anonymous writings should not be indiscriminately passed around anyway.

Second, company officials or executives may believe that they have knowledge of the author of such notes. Undoubtedly, when a hostile or threatening note is received, employers ponder who might be the writer of such a document and may make their own assessments as to the person's identity. This can be premature, especially if action such as dismissal is taken. Employers and human resource personnel should wait until the identity of the author is determined and proof is supplied before drawing conclusions and taking action. Such premature steps might very well result in a lawsuit for wrongful termination, a situation everyone wishes to avoid. So, above all, do not take action based on a mere supposition about guilt or innocence.

An example of jumping to wrongful conclusions: last year a company owner called me and informed me that he had a threatening note, that he knew who the author was, and that he had already terminated the employee. He wanted me to examine the note just for "verification." When I called him to let him know my results, he was highly agitated and surprised by the fact that he had identified and fired the wrong person! Can you say "wrongful termination lawsuit"?

When presenting a document problem to me, people often say, "I'm not a handwriting expert, but even I can see the similarities." However, these similarities that they see might only be "class characteristics"—generic handwriting features that are common to vast groups of writers—rather than distinctive handwriting characteristics indicative of one specific person. Some people do have a natural ability to distinguish distinctive handwriting similarities; others do not. In fact, some people are "form blind" and cannot perceive handwriting differences at all. Although signatures and writing styles may look similar to the casual viewer, only an experienced handwriting expert should be used to determine authorship of notes.

Having participated in many EEO meetings as both a state and federal government employee, and having worked anonymous document cases brought to me by owners and managers of many companies, large and small, I have seen two perspectives on anonymous writings.

The Company's Perspective:

Harassing, threatening, or sexually harassing anonymous writings put companies in a difficult situation. If they do nothing, they can be held liable for inaction, particularly if the note leaver were to carry out his threat, whether by setting off a bomb or raping a fellow employee. How-ever, if the company acts abruptly and dismisses a suspected wrongdoer without sufficient cause, they will have a wrongful termination claim against them, and they will be talking to union representatives and attor-neys.

As an employer, then, realize that you are on the brink of potential civil and criminal proceedings. This is a fine line that employers must walk. They need to exercise extreme thoughtfulness, yet balanced deci-siveness, as they proceed. In order to proceed properly when confronted by an anonymous writing, it helps if the company has a written SOP that has been thoroughly examined by an attorney specializing in labor law in your state.

The Employee's Perspective:

Employees have the right to perform their daily tasks free from threats of physical harm, intimidation, or even stalking. So when harassment really takes place, employers need to protect victim claimants right away, working with the claimant to ensure his or her immediate safety as well as a productive working environment. However, the suspect has rights too. Those rights must be preserved until legitimate evidence develops against him or her.

Two possibilities always exist: either the claimant is truly being ha-rassed, or the claimant is the one creating the anonymous document. Why would a person do such a thing? Either to set up another employee in the hope of getting someone else fired, or perhaps merely to get atten-tion for himself. In such cases the claimant may place a note after having written the suspect's name on it. For this reason, if documents are going to be submitted to a Forensic Document Examiner for analysis, hand-writing samples should be obtained from the suspect, the claimant vic-tim, and various other employees who work in the same area where the note was found.

The following paragraphs give more detail regarding the different types of anonymous notes and may help you define your action should someone in your company receive one.

Generally Harassing Notes

In a small valley town lived a mother of three children who had pre-viously had problems getting along with her neighbor. She called the local police department and had a detective come out to investigate an anonymous harassing letter she claimed to have received in her porch mailbox. She claimed that the note had been written by a neighbor. After the visit from the detective, she received more anonymous notes, and they became more provocative. In fact, one of the anonymous messages was a composite letter, made up of word fragments cut out of magazines and glued to a sheet of paper. When this composite page was sent to me for examination, I turned the sheet over and processed the reverse blank side to see if there were any latent handwriting impressions that might have been left from a previous page laid over the top. (See the discussion on "latent writing" in Chapter 2.)

When I processed the sheet, I noticed that someone had written a "to do" list on a previous sheet of paper from the same tablet. It revealed such highlights as going to the store and picking the kids up from school. This latent writing established that the "victim" had been creating these anonymous messages herself. I reported my findings to the detective. This mother of three later confessed, revealing that she had wanted the attention of the detective and had also wanted to get her neighbor into trouble. Although she could have been arrested for submitting a false police report, she was let go with a warning.

Sexually Harassing Notes

Such notes can be a form of stalking from people too shy to actually talk to the person they admire, or they may be notes that border on lewdness or even contain threats of bodily harm. These anonymous messages can simply be an annoyance to the recipients, or they may cause them sleepless nights of terror. Sexually harassing notes might be left on a person's car windshield, locker, or desk, or they may come through inter-office mail or regular U.S. mail. In the latter case, the matter becomes a federal crime.

Death Threats or Threats of Assault

In the wake of the Columbine High School massacre, the word went out that all threats of bodily harm should be taken very seriously and even brought to the attention of local law enforcement. Employers should drop everything else they are doing and address such issues immediately. In my own practice, I always put crimes or threats against persons at the top of my list, working them immediately and cooperating with companies and law enforcement agencies to get an answer as quickly as possible.

This is true not only for death threats, but also for sabotage notes, bomb threats, and sexually harassing notes.

In these situations I don't believe it is enough to simply turn matters over to law enforcement and then forget about it. Not only should you as the employer maintain full cooperation with the police agency you turned the matter over to, but you should also keep a watchful eye in the workplace, seeking information to aid in apprehending the culprit.

Sabotage Notes and Bomb Threats

Sabotage can be defined as "the destruction of property to obstruct normal operations" or "treacherous action to defeat or hinder an endeavor." If the sabotage threatened in the note does occur, the company itself is the potential victim, but innocent bystanders may also become victims if anything breaks or explodes. Any anonymous writings that refer to sabotage or bomb threats should be taken seriously, and your local law enforcement agency should be contacted immediately.

If you have received such threats, be on the lookout for unmetered mail packages or packages in unusual places, which could contain mercury switches. Such bombs explode only when picked up. Other packages may contain timing devices and may explode at a preordained time. When confronted with such lone packages, you should contact the Federal Bureau of Alcohol, Tobacco, and Firearms, who know how to deal with such deadly devices. Figure 15.1 depicts a typical bomb threat note.

Preserving an Anonymous Document

If you have received an anonymous note, immediately take the following steps to preserve the note, as well as any envelope that may have come with it:

1. Wearing cloth gloves, pick up the anonymous document and gently place it in a protective plastic document cover, then put it inside two hard-stock file folders. Place these in a 10" x 13" clasp envelope. Do not write over the top of these file folders or the envelope.

2. Do not touch the note or allow any other person to touch it. If the person who found the note did happen to handle it, make a note of where he or she touched it, as well as the names of anyone else who may have touched or handled the note.

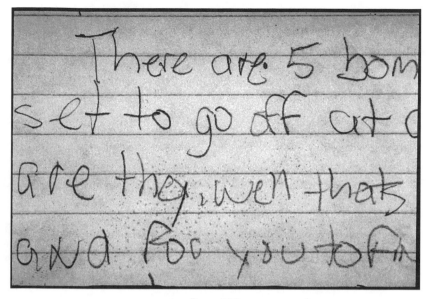

Figure 15.1

Figure 15.1 depicts a bomb threat note. The serviceman who left this note on an Air Force base was court martialed.

3. Write down the exact time the note was found and the location in the company, ie. on a desk, in a drawer, pinned or taped to a wall, etc.

4. If the message was written on a wall, mirror, door, or other such surface with grease pen, lipstick, spray paint, or felt marker, these surfaces should be properly photographed and the photos developed before cleaning such surfaces. I would suggest the following steps:

   a) call the local police or sheriff's department and file an incident report. Request that they send out identification technicians to process the scene, but before they appear,

   b) take your own photographs and have them developed right away. If you don't like the results, you can return with a professional photographer who will know how to shoot the surface using proper lighting, film, and filters.

Taking your own photographs may help if the police identification section does less than a first-rate job taking the pictures. With no disrespect intended against law enforcement agencies, in cases such as these, I have sometimes been supplied with mediocre to poor-quality photographs by law enforcement personnel.

Investigative Steps

There are several steps that should be taken when investigating the authorship of an anonymous writing. If you are going to insist on treating the incident as an internal business matter, then you need to know how to proceed. If you involve law enforcement in the incident, realize that most police agencies have not had much experience with anonymous writings and therefore don't know all of the issues involved in investigating them. The following suggestions can be used as a checklist for yourself as well as for the detective who has been assigned to your case.

If the anonymous note was handwritten:

1. Go through time cards and try to determine who was working on or around the time the note was believed to have been left. Obtain handwriting specimens of suspects from their work product and from their employee files. Suspects include people who work in the immediate area, the person who found the anonymous writing, and also the person to whom it was addressed.

2. Submit the original note, along with known writings by any suspects, to a legitimate Questioned Document Examiner. This examiner should conduct a handwriting comparison to determine whether any of the suspects did or did not write the anonymous document.

3. The document should also be processed to detect the presence of any latent handwriting impressions (discussed in Chapter 2). If you contact a Questioned Document Examiner or "handwriting expert" who seems unclear as to what latent writing examinations are, or if he or she does not have a machine that can develop latent writing images, seek another expert!

4. The anonymous note may contain the fingerprints of the

writer, so a fingerprint examination should be considered, but it should only be performed after the examination by the Questioned Document Examiner.

If the anonymous note was typewritten or computer generated:

1. Submit the original anonymous note to a Questioned Document Examiner. An initial microscopic examination of the typed characters will determine whether the note was made by a typewriter or by a computer printer.

2. If the document was made by a typewriter, then typing samples on suspect machines should be obtained. Paper found at the suspect workstations should be used. The person taking the sample should type the exact text as it appears on the questioned anonymous note, working from a photocopy. He should first type, "This is a typing exemplar." This will avoid confusion of the sample text with the actual questioned text. After typing the exact text, the operator should also type, "End of typing exemplar." Then include the date and initials or name of the operator typing the sample. The operator should then hand-initial and date the page and also write down which machine was used to prepare the sample and also which typing element (ball).

3. The ribbon cartridge should be removed from that machine, placed in a plastic bag, and placed in a larger envelope along with the typed sample pages from that machine. These should then be submitted to the Questioned Document Examiner for analysis.

4. If the document was prepared by a computer printer, explore only those computers connected to the same type of printer, whether laser, ink-jet, or dot-matrix.

5. Data string search command matches should be conducted on any suspect computer hard drives in an effort to find the matching text of the anonymous note. If a match can be found, then you have at least isolated the computer and workstation on which the note was created, and you will also have time and date stamp information of the file, which

may assist in the investigation. Keep in mind, however, that just because you have identified the computer that generated the anonymous note, does not mean that the employee who works at that desk is indeed the writer. Nonetheless, that employee should be at the top of the suspect list.

6. Fingerprint and latent handwriting examinations of the anonymous note should be performed.

In all cases involving anonymous notes, two types of examinations should always be considered, and they should be conducted in strict order. First, questioned document examinations should be performed, which involve handwriting comparisons, mechanical impression examinations, paper examination, latent handwriting tests, and any other forensic document examinations deemed appropriate for the given evidence. After all questioned document examinations have been conducted, fingerprint examinations should then be performed.

There is a difference between "latent fingerprints" and "inked fingerprints." A latent fingerprint is the invisible print left on the surface as a result of touching an item, whether it be a doorknob, the window or side panel of a car, a gun, a "blunt instrument," or a knife. When we touch non-porous surfaces, we usually leave our fingerprints on them. However, many people do not know that when they handle a piece of paper, whether a letter-size sheet, envelope, or paper fragment, they can also leave their fingerprints or palm prints on it.

"Inked fingerprints" are placed directly on a fingerprint card, which goes on file with a law enforcement agency. These inked fingerprints are taken for various reasons. Anyone who is arrested is fingerprinted when "booked." All California teachers are fingerprinted. When a person gets a driver's license from the California Department of Motor Vehicles, he or she gives the department a thumbprint. Many other states do the same.

Approximately one-third of the California population has been fingerprinted. In fact, ten million fingerprint cards are on file just at the California Department of Justice. Although other states are behind those numbers, new legislation is mandating that their agencies maintain fingerprint cards on their residents who apply for certain government positions and other jobs. Consequently, inked fingerprint and palm print cards do exist for many people. The benefit in working with law enforcement agencies is that they have the legal ability to obtain such fingerprint cards on individuals under investigation.

Keep in mind, however, that some people are not "secretors," and their fingerprints may not show up on documents even though they have handled them. Further, savvy anonymous note writers may use gloves when preparing the note. Therefore, just because a person's fingerprints are not on a document, does not mean that he or she did not handle it.

Aiding Law Enforcement Investigations

Some law enforcement agencies actually skip any questioned document examinations and only process the document for fingerprints. There are several possible reasons for this. It may be that they don't have people in their forensic laboratory that do questioned document work, or there is a long wait to have questioned document work performed by the few agencies available to them that do it. Many law enforcement personnel are also unaware that latent writing images can be revealed on paper.

Also, when processing documents to develop fingerprints on them, many law enforcement agencies use old processing methods and chemicals that cause inks to run and at times virtually destroy the evidence. The modern chemical used in processing documents for the presence of any fingerprints is ninhydrin with a hexane base. The old formula still being used by many agencies today is ninhydrin with an acetone base. The problem with acetone as a base for ninhydrin is that it causes a lot of inks to run or even to vanish. If the identification technician failed to photograph or at least photocopy the original document before processing it, the evidence is gone.

Law enforcement agencies that use outdated methods often do so because hexane is more expensive. This practice is penny wise and pound foolish. Having worked both civil and criminal cases from around the United States, I have seen that many law enforcement agencies seem to do good investigative work with almost everything else but paper.

For the record, the California State Department of Justice Bureau of Forensic Services, as well as the established Federal Forensic Crime Laboratories, in addition to many larger agencies such as the Los Angeles Sheriff's Office, the Arizona Department of Public Safety, and the Colorado Bureau of Criminal Investigation, all have the policy that documents under investigation go to the Questioned Document Section first, where analysts wear gloves while handling the evidence. Only after these examinations are completed do these documents go on to the Latent

Fingerprint sections for fingerprint examination. These agencies know the potential value of questioned document work. A number of small law enforcement agencies around the country do not. When I am on the defense side of such cases, I always look for and bring to light any shoddy work by investigators or specialists who cut corners and/or use improper or outdated methods.

As the employer, you can at least point out to the detective handling your case what you understand should be done. Have it on record, including what detective or official you told, as well as the time and date, and try to have a witness standing by that you can note in the file as well. Although the detectives may take offense to you checking up on how they do their job, at least your concerns will have been expressed. If anything should go awry concerning the fingerprint examination or the questioned document examination, you, as the company representative, will be on record as having done everything in your power to help the investigation proceed correctly.

It is common for emotions to run wild when anonymous writings are found. Balanced justice will prevail, however, if the recommendations in this chapter and these general common-sense guidelines are followed.

Checklist: General Recommendations Regarding Anonymous Writings

1. Handle anonymous documents so as not to damage them or leave your fingerprints.

2. If the anonymous writings are threatening in any way, call the police.

3. Consider the potential value of questioned document and fingerprint examinations.

4. Consider the potential value of hard drive searches of suspect computers.

5. Do not terminate or suspend suspected employees without good reason.

6. Remind employees during staff meetings about the impropriety of leaving anonymous notes.

7. Consider installing surveillance cameras and warning employees about their presence as a deterrence against anonymous notes.

SIXTEEN

WHEN FRAUD HAS
ALREADY OCCURED

Systematic Solutions for Damage Control

Perhaps you or someone you know has fallen victim to one of the scams already described in this book. There are several things you should know and do if you have been defrauded. Much of the following amounts to the same advice I give to people who call me every day. Here are the procedures to follow when others have committed fraud against you.

First, start a folder which begins with what I call a "chrono" sheet. While it's fresh in your mind, write down everything that happens and what steps you are taking along the way. Keep track of events, dates, witnesses, phone calls, and meetings, as well as what people say during any of these discussions.

Be sure to protect any documents involved in the matter. Place your originals and best copies of the documents in a file folder, and limit how much you handle them. Don't give anything away to anybody else, including the police, without asking a lot of questions. It's possible that your evidence will get lost in the police system. If at all possible, give copies, not originals, to other interested parties. If you must give up your best evidence, first make a photocopy and a color copy, as well as scanning it to a high resolution file, say 300 dpi.

Depending on what happened, you may first want to file a police incident report and have them give you an incident report number.

Whether or not the police detectives will come and interview you depends on if the event was criminal in nature. A good way to find out is to call the Financial Crimes Bureau or the Robbery/Theft Bureau of your local law enforcement killer agency and tell them what happened. If they deem the incident "a civil matter," they will not help you at this point, and you will have to get your own attorney.

However, many proceedings start as civil matters but, as evidence develops, turn into criminal matters. You may have to push the investigation along—not for the purpose of forcing your incident into the criminal arena, but simply because if you don't nurture your case, no one else will. Whether you "turn it over" to detectives or a civil attorney, remember, the squeaky wheel gets the grease. You will have to keep calling these people to keep your case prominent in their minds. Both detectives and attorneys are not only busy, but usually overwhelmed, so reminders will be in order if you want to see progress.

If you need an attorney, make sure you retain one with experience in the appropriate area for your needs. For example, if you are trying to enforce a contract on which your opponent is denying his signature in an effort to get out of a contractual obligation, then retain an attorney who is well versed in business contract law. Don't get an attorney who specializes in family law unless that is the area at issue. Ask other people you know for a referral, including other business persons. When you interview attorneys, ask them about their schedules and whether or not they can handle your case. Many are the attorneys who are quick to take the retainer, but are slow to return your calls. Make sure that you feel comfortable that this attorney will take an active interest in your case.

Once you line up your attorney, he or she may very well need to retain a Questioned Document Examiner to review the case documents. Since most attorneys that I deal with have not had previous experience working with a Questioned Document Examiner, what follows is a discussion of the field of forensic document examination to help you and your attorney better understand how it relates to your case.

Questioned Document Examination

The field of questioned document examination has a long tradition, encompassing such famous investigations and cases as the Howard Hughes will, the Zodiac killer, the Unabomber case, and the Charles Lindbergh baby kidnapping trial. Questioned document testimony has been accepted by the U.S. courts for over one hundred years. Albert S. Osborn, with the publication of his book *Questioned Documents* in 1910, is credited with laying the academic foundation of this field of scientific forensic investigation.

Perhaps one of the most significant affirming nods to the questioned document field comes from all of the government laboratories that continue to employ full-time Questioned Document Examiners—such agencies as the Federal Bureau of Investigation, the Immigration and Naturalization Service, the United States Secret Service, the Central Intelligence Agency, the Internal Revenue Service, and the Bureau of Alcohol, Tobacco, and Firearms. Beyond these there are the many state and county laboratories that employ Questioned Document Examiners not only for investigations, but also to testify in court as expert witnesses.

The Work of Questioned Document Examiners

Questioned (or "Forensic") Document Examiners are involved primarily in determining whether handwriting is authentic or forged and in identifying who did or did not produce a particular writing. Questioned handwriting and signatures can be compared to examples of a suspect's everyday "known" writings to determine whether or not the suspect wrote the entries in question. Comparisons can be conducted concerning signatures and initials, cursive handwriting (longhand), hand printing, block printing, and numbers. These examinations are applied to a wide variety of documents, such as wills, deeds, legal contracts, checks, medical records, insurance records, anonymous documents, and court documents.

In addition to examining handwriting, forensic document examiners may also deal with documents that have been typewritten, computer printed, or photocopied. "Questioned" documents may be forged, counterfeited, or altered; and examiners can often reconstruct charred documents or latent impressions on documents as well.

"QD" Examiners also render expert opinions regarding other aspects of documents, such as typewriting, paper, ink, and printing processes. Work in this field may include deciphering alterations and erasures or revealing latent handwriting impressions on paper. These processes generate hard evidence in determining the identity of anonymous writers of threatening or lewd notes (see chapter 15) or in determining if bogus inserted pages were placed into wills, trusts, employee files, or medical records. Dating a document, determining what is written under an obliteration, and differentiating between inks is also work within the scope of this profession.

By the way, Questioned Document Examiners don't usually like using the "f" word—"forgery." The reason is that when one person signs the name of another person, that signature will have been executed under one of two possible conditions. If I give permission for another person to sign my own name, that signature is not a forgery. However, if someone signs my name without my knowledge or my permission, then he or she is doing so for the purpose of deception and fraud. The word "forgery," then, indicates that the intent of the "forger" was to defraud.

For a QD Examiner to say that a signature is forged implies that he has reason to believe that he understands the frame of mind of the forger. It is difficult to know the situation and the frame of mind of a person writing a name, whether it is his or her own name or that of another person. So for this reason, QD examiners try to avoid using the "f" word; however, it does provide for convenient shorthand when discussing the situation. That is, instead of saying,

"The questioned signature does not exhibit the natural, normal nor genuine handwriting characteristics of Madame X and therefore was written by someone other than Madame X,"

it becomes convenient and easily understood by most people to simply say,

"The signature was forged."

In any litigation concerning questioned documents, there are always two matters to address. First, what is the "question" concerning the questioned document? If it is a matter of handwriting (or hand printing), then what kind of handwriting? Is it merely a question of a single signature? Are initials in question? Or are only some handwritten numbers at issue?

If the question concerns handwriting, then control documents must be obtained. That is, if we are going to do a comparison of questioned handwriting, then we must have a sample of the person's true handwriting. I have seen attorneys agonize over trying to obtain handwriting samples by certain persons. Usually the obtaining of handwriting specimens seems to be a difficult task because investigators don't know where to look, so I have included here a sampling of ideas from a handout I have called "Sources of Signatures and Handwriting":

Driver's licenses, identification cards, court documents, fingerprint cards, canceled checks, employment applications, marriage licenses, fishing or hunting licenses, rental agreements, military records, insurance policies, passports, tax returns, bank signature cards, canceled payroll checks, personnel jackets, letters, diaries, notebooks, address books, recipes, receipts, hotel/motel registration cards, pawn tickets.

"Forensic Document Examination"

The word "forensic" means "the application of science to law." So whether it is DNA testing, trace evidence, firearm and tool mark analysis ("ballistics"), odontology (teeth) or pathology (dead bodies), these are scientific fields that attempt to uncover evidence that would be of evidentiary significance in a civil or criminal court of law. "Forensic Questioned Document Examination," then, is the examination of documents using the scientific method in order to develop evidence that will assist the tryers of fact (the jurors or the judge in a "bench trial") in rendering a verdict.

The Scientific Method

Some fondle crystal balls, others throw chicken bones, but as a Questioned Document Examiner, I use the scientific method to work through document problems. I have heard people explain that "Questioned Document Examination is a combination of both science and art." Although that sounds nice, I'm not really sure what it means. On the one hand, I am by no means an artist or an art critic, unless you call stick men and doodling "art." Neither am I a scientist in the sense that you can find zapping antennas and boiling caldrons in my office.

However, as I recall from my high school science classes, the scientific method employs hypothesis, experimentation, observation, and the recording of results. These results should be repeatable by other similarly-trained and experienced technicians using the same materials and the same procedures under the same conditions.

So in any document problem, there is a hypothesis, such as "Mr. x did sign this document" or "Mr. x did not sign this document." Data is then collected to perform a meaningful examination in an effort to arrive at a conclusion. The results obtained should be repeatable by others of the same training and experience using the same evidence and methodologies. (See Selecting a Qualified QD Examiner below.)

When I am testifying in court, some attorneys for the opponent think it's a neat trap to ask me, "Is Questioned Document Examination an exact science?" Of course, they are trying to make me look bad no matter what answer I give. It's like the old question, "Have you stopped beating your wife?" If I say "no, it is not an exact science," then they can pounce on my answer and equate my work to chicken bones and crystal balls. If I answer "yes," then they try to disprove my answer by focusing on the interpretive side of my field. One of the ways I like to answer this question is with the response, "Even in the 'exact science' of mathematics, the conclusions are only as exact as the mathematician." And I further point out that, while I do apply the scientific method in my examinations, I am not an educated or trained scientist in the strict sense.

Furthermore, although the field does not fall under the strict definitions of "science," Questioned Document Examiners are indeed considered "skilled technicians." They are likened to harbor pilots, who by virtue of their specialized training and experience, know the currents, eddies, and sandbars and are valuable pointers of the way. Therefore, they may offer expert witnesses testimony to assist the jury under Federal Rule 702 concerning expert witnesses in court.

During my discussions with attorneys, I usually find that they are not familiar with the significance, terminology, and investigative procedures of questioned document examination. They usually admit that this is the first time they have ever used a Questioned Document Examiner. This, in part, prompted me to write a technical paper as to the nature of handwriting identification. For the convenience of you and your attorney, this paper has been edited and reprinted at the end of this book under Appendix B.

Questioned Document Examination and Litigation

I have also learned that attorneys are unfamiliar with case law pertaining to the field of questioned documents. Since the case law itself is so extensive, I have not reproduced any in this book. Suffice it to say here that hundreds of court rulings have been made with regard to the admissibility of forensic document examinations in U.S. courts. There are two general categories of litigation that pertain to questioned document examinations: criminal and civil.

Criminal Litigation

There was a married couple who were burglarized while they were away during the day. The woman returned home, drove into the garage, and closed the garage door behind her. When she entered the house, the burglar accosted her and tied her to the bed. As the day went on, he would alternate between raping her and rummaging through the kitchen to eat, then loading up their vehicle with loot. The husband finally returned home, and he too was surprised and tied to a chair. The burglar took the couple's ATM and credit cards, forcing his victims to tell him their PIN numbers. When night fell, the burglar drove off in their vehicle and stopped at ATM machines to get cash.

This parolee was the boyfriend of the couple's house cleaner, who supplied the burglar with the house key and a schematic of the house showing where all the valuables were. Both the burglar and the house cleaner were picked up on suspicion, and this matter went to court. I was able to identify the house cleaner as the person who wrote the schematic, and she then turned state's evidence against the burglar. I was also able to identify the burglar as the person who wrote the PIN number information on a piece of paper. This burglar/rapist was sentenced to ninety years in prison.

I also had a murder case in which the suspect wrote a death threat on the victim's bathroom mirror to terrorize her just before killing her. The message was written in red lipstick and was difficult to photograph, since other objects reflected in the image while I was trying to take the picture of the writing on the mirror itself. Using a combination of filters and photography techniques, however, I was able to prepare enlarged photos to take to the jury. After the suspect was located and extradited from Mexico, he stood trial. Using known writings from letters he had formerly sent to the victim, I was able to identify him as the writer of the murder message on the mirror. This, of course, showed premeditation and laid the foundation for criminal sentencing.

Although some criminal prosecution cases involving questioned documents are crimes against persons, the majority of them are property crimes. In one example, there was a burglar who was caught leaving a residence through the bedroom window with a bag of loot in his hand. The police suspected that he had probably committed the burglary next door as well, which had been pulled off a few nights before. In that previous burglary, the burglar wrote messages all over the walls, doors, a painting, and a bathroom mirror. The detectives went to his jail cell with butcher paper and taped it to the wall, then told the suspect to write. They dictated the same messages that had been written in the home of the first burglary victim. On the basis of these known handwriting samples taken by the police, I was able to identify this suspect as the person who wrote in the first victim's house (see Figure 16.1).

Graffiti is a type of property crime since it vandalizes and devalues property. Investigation of graffiti offers its own challenges for several reasons. First, the writing surfaces, such as train cars, buildings, equipment, and fences and other structures, are almost always vertical and abnormal from the standpoint of their differences from paper. Another challenge in working with graffiti is that the writing instrument is unusual—normally a can of spray paint, markers, etc.

Many graffiti writings are artistic in nature. They can be mostly handwriting or "bubble writing," or they can be mostly art, or a combination.

Figure 16.1

When graffiti are composed more of artistic drawings than of writings, the Document Examiner cannot do much with them because they do not exhibit natural handwriting habits of the writer, and it is natural writing that we use to identify and eliminate suspect writers. The key to identifying the writer of graffiti is to find known samples of the person's graffiti style of handwriting. This has been done on numerous occasions by obtaining papers from the suspect's bedroom, school binders, and vehicles.

And finally, there are the everyday forgery and embezzlement cases that, although technically criminal in nature, are not always accepted by many law enforcement agencies unless they involve a high-enough dollar amount. Although forgery is, of course, a crime, some law enforcement agencies receive so many cases of this type that they set dollar amount thresholds to determine which cases will be pursued. In some of these situations, your business may be able to lump a group of forged or embezzled checks together in an effort to meet the minimum dollar threshold needed for your local law enforcement agency to take the case. If the mail was used by the perpetrators in some way, this would offer you grounds to talk to the local Postal Inspector, who may pursue the case as a federal crime.

Civil Litigation

Much of this type of questioned document litigation relates to probate issues involving wills, codicils, and trusts. This subject is discussed in detail in Chapter 12. Probate most often creates problems for the elderly, who need to put safeguards in place to protect themselves when still alive, and to protect their estates after they pass on.

Questioned document examination often comes into play in family law issues. One popular ploy in custody disputes is to plant threatening messages, supposedly from the other spouse, in an effort to show the court how unstable that parent is so that full custody will be awarded to the "sane" parent. Another angle on this is to plant a note which portrays a parent as a child molester or murderer, then bring this to the court's attention. These notes or letters should be handled from the same standpoint as anonymous notes in the workplace, as discussed in Chapter 15.

There was one such note, supposedly left by the father, instructing the son to "get the gun" and blow his mother's brains out. The mother finished off this scheme by going around to the neighbors and having them write glowing references as to what a balanced, loving, perfect mother and neighbor she had been! Handwriting examinations revealed that it was the mother, not the father, who had written this note.

The Care and Marking of Questioned Documents

As soon as a document is identified as "questioned"—that is, it becomes the subject of some controversy—it should be immediately safeguarded according to the following points. Although you may think that some of these steps will not be necessary, let me point out that at the beginning of any investigation, you will not be sure which examinations should or should not be conducted. It will only take a few additional minutes to comply with all of the suggestions listed below, and by doing so you will preserve the record for any and all examinations that may become necessary down the line.

1. Protect the document. Immediately place any questioned document in a file folder, then place the file folder inside a larger clasp envelope. This will preserve the document from additional fingerprints and from wear, and it will reduce the possibility of the document receiving any additional latent handwriting impressions.

2. Questioned documents and known samples should not be folded, stapled, or paper clipped to anything. If you need to keep groups of documents together, put them in clasp envelopes.

3. It is best not to mark on a questioned document in any way. If you need to identify it, you can write whatever you need to on the clasp envelope that you have placed it in. However, remove the questioned document from the clasp envelope before writing on it, as your writings may penetrate onto the questioned document inside and may confuse a latent handwriting examination if one becomes necessary.

4. When pointing out details on a document as you discuss the case with pertinent people, avoid touching the document with a pencil, pen, pointed instrument, or any object which might damage or deface it. I can't tell you how many times I have cringed as people have pointed to different areas of a questioned document with a gooping pen as they take me on an odyssey through their case. I have had to ask clients to "please put the pen down" because I became so concerned that I couldn't concentrate on what they were telling me. Such innocently placed markings can become huge distractions during litigation.

5. Documents that have been damaged by tearing, cutting, water, or fire should be submitted for examination in the same condition as when recovered. Make no attempt to repair or restore them.

Damaging of Documents During Examination

Since the vast majority of document problems are solved with microscopic, photographic, electrostatic, and imaging techniques, the documents are not damaged or defaced during an examination. However, in the rare event it would become necessary to damage a document, even though the damage would be minute, permission should always be obtained from all parties ahead of time.

An example of this might occur when there is an intersection of a typewritten character with a portion of a signature line, and the question is, "What hit the paper first, the signature or the typed text?" To answer this question, the examiner can remove a microscopic portion of the carbon film of the ribbon to see what is underneath (see the figure of the large "E" on page 39). Even though the portion of typewriter ribbon ink removed would be undetectable to the naked eye, it is still proper etiquette for the examiner to request permission to perform such a procedure.

Selecting a Qualified Forensic Document Expert

If you find that you need the services of a Questioned Document Examiner, then you should do your homework. If you do an Internet search of "handwriting expert" or "forged signature" or "questioned documents," you will find a host of so-called "Questioned Document Examiners." Some will be properly-trained, legitimate document examiners. Others will be charlatans—people who call themselves QD Examiners but who are not competent to handle your case. They will all appear legitimate, however, since they have studied the advertisements of legitimate examiners so as to know what types of things to say. The following guidelines will help you select a competent and qualified Questioned Document Examiner.

Look for these credentials:

1. **Present or former experience as a full time Questioned Document Examiner (or "Analyst")**

   This is the single best way to ensure that you are getting a legitimate questioned document expert. Make sure that he or she has spent time as a full-time Questioned Document Examiner government agency employee performing only forensic questioned document work. However, be cautious of persons who imply full-time past service as a QD examiner employee. When an inquiry call was made about one such person who strongly implied that his federal job was as a Questioned Document Examiner, it was discovered that this "expert" had indeed been a federal government employee: a janitor.

Many charlatans will try to imply government experience by talking about a case they did for the local sheriff's department or the local district attorney's office. Many unsuspecting detectives or deputy DA's have made snap decisions on an "expert" who was not really qualified, and thereafter that so-called expert will use such casework to boast that he has "government experience" and is "court qualified." The truth of the matter is that each and every court we appear before as experts must qualify us as an expert to appear before that particular court of law.

2. Proper training and experience

Have the person you contacted fax you his or her "CV" (Curriculum Vitae), which is a type of resume. There is no good reason why he or she should hesitate to send you a copy. Upon receipt, you need to carefully consider its content. First of all, does the CV refer to a training period? If so, was the training in Europe? This is a favorite trick of charlatans in the United States, since they think nobody will bother to check out their overseas training. However, one such "expert" was called to account by the U.S. Attorney in San Francisco. This "expert" claimed training in Europe, but when the European institution was contacted, they informed the U.S. Attorney's office that this person had never even been enrolled in their school; moreover, they had no training or degree program in Questioned Document Examinations. The local court imposed sanctions against this so-called expert.

Questioned Document training is something like Jedi training, only it doesn't take as long. The Jedis of Star Wars fame are supposedly apprenticed from young childhood until adulthood. The field of Questioned Document Examination requires a minimum of two years of full-time training, during which the apprentice works under the scrutiny of a recognized journey-level Questioned Document Examiner. During these two years the examiner trainee studies the basic literature, completes study projects, and learns about forensic sciences in general and questioned documents in particular in the legal system.

The most important part of this training, however, occurs when the trainee is taken through hundreds of actual questioned document cases. This field cannot be learned through correspondence courses; hands-on experience is necessary. Only when the QD trainer believes his apprentice is ready will he cut him or her loose to render independent conclusions regarding forensic document cases. The Examiner you are considering should be able to name the person who was responsible for his or her training. Bona fide examiners should be able to explain the lineage through which their training was obtained.

The other element to consider is longevity. Just because a "Questioned Document Expert" claims many years in the field, this does not equate to competence. I would trust a properly trained Questioned Document Examiner with only a few years under his or her belt before entrusting an important matter to a "veteran" who was never properly trained in the first place. Such incompetent "experts" simply repeat mistakes over time since they lacked the proper foundation to begin with.

3. Professional Memberships

Your questioned documents expert should belong to government recognized forensic document organizations, such as the Southwestern Association of Forensic Document Examiners (SWAFDE), the American Society of Questioned Document Examiners (ASQDE), or the Questioned Document Section of the American Academy of Forensic Sciences (AAFS).

4. Certification

The examiner you are considering should be Certified by the American Board of Forensic Document Examiners (the "A.B.F.D.E."). The A.B.F.D.E. began in 1977, sponsored by the American Academy of Forensic Sciences, the American Society of Questioned Document Examiners, and the Canadian Society of Forensic Science. The A.B.F.D.E. has a thorough application and testing procedure to ensure the proper background and competence of its Diplomates. Be cautious of other Boards with similar-sounding names, but who really only credential their members by means of limited correspondence schools for money and who do not require the proper, full-time journeyman-apprentice training.

5. **Court Experience**

Ask to see the examiner's list of court appearances in the last four years. Expert witnesses who testify in federal court (civil) are supposed to provide a list of what cases they have testified in over the past four years. He or she should have qualified in the courtroom as an expert witness numerous times, although some phony experts embellish or lie about their courtroom experience. If the "expert" balks about showing you the list, then call someone else. If you are provided a list, I advise contacting a few of the attorneys and/or courts on it to verify some random instances.

Unfortunately, there are a lot of people lying out there, so be careful and do your homework. Since it is difficult to receive training in questioned document analysis, legitimate and qualified QD examiners can only be numbered in the hundreds rather than in the thousands. As a matter of fact, at this writing, only 150 QD examiners are certified by the American Board of Forensic Document Examiners (the A.B.F.D.E), the only legitimate certifying board.

Where to Find Legitimate Q.D. Examiners

Although I cannot vouch for the complete competency of each and every listed person on the following web site, I will say that I know many of these people and respect their work. I feel that you are in good hands when contacting these persons with your fraud problems. The A.B.F.D.E. maintains a web site at http://www.abfde.org, where they list by state certified QD Examiners so you can locate a Questioned Document Examiner near you.

GLOSSARY/INDEX

advance fee scam, p. 124

alteration, p. 6

arbitration hearing—a legal proceeding in which two opposing sides put forth their arguments, witnesses, and evidence before a hearing officer or judge. Although more informal than a courtroom setting, it is similar to a "bench trial" in which a judge hears the case and then rules on the outcome. pp. 129, 161, 165

authentic—the true, correct or real signature, document, stamp impression, or other manifestation of the document. pp. 4, 61, 83, 199

back-ups, computer data, p. 167

bond paper—plain, generic paper devoid of watermarks or special textures or designs. pp. 16, 163

check writer (ie. a Paymaster)—a machine which stamps the legal amount of money on the face of the check. pp. 6, 69

class characteristics—those handwriting features common to vast groups of writers. Copy book forms as depicted in grade school handwriting charts on the wall, which are devoid of individual handwriting distinctiveness. p. 185

codicil—a supplement to a preexisting will that changes portions of it. p. 137

composite document—a two-part document with at least one of the portions being a cut-and-paste recycling of a portion of another (legitimate) document. p. 15

decedent—in probate, the person who has died. p. 139

contemporaneous—of the same time period, used here in reference to the comparisons of known documents which are from around the same time period as the document in question. p. 33

controller's warrant—a check issued by a government office to a public assistance (welfare) recipient. pp. 4, 61, 68

counter check—blank checks available at the bank counter for use with any customer account. p. 66

counterfeit—an imitation designed to pass as an original, or the unauthorized duplication of a negotiable instrument with the intent to defraud. pp. 3, 50, 79, 83

debit card, pp. 89, 123

deed of trust, or "trust deed," p. 131

dot-matrix printer—an older style of computer printer that uses tiny pins in a housing that strike against an ink ribbon to leave alphanumeric characters on the printed page. pp. 51, 52, 191

e-mail spoofing, p. 179

embezzle—"to take fraudulently in violation of a trust." Used of bookkeepers who steal from the company using any number of methods described in this book. pp. xx, 8, 45, 50

endorsement signature—the signature of the payee on back side of a check. p. 63

epiphanies—used here to mean "miraculous appearances" of mysterious signatures. p. 35

escrow—the process of legally transferring the title of a property from the former to the new owner. pp. 131, 134

e-signature, pp. 29, 180

executor—the person designated to probate the estate left by the deceased. pp. 141, 143

exemplar—a handwriting sample given for the express purpose of comparing it to a specific questioned document. p. 14

expert witness—a trained and experienced specialist in any field who testifies his or her findings in a court of law. pp. 199, 202

extraneous toner marks—small blotches printed on a document as the result of defects in the reproduction processes of a photocopy machine. p. 15

FAT—"**File Allocation Table,**" p. 166

firewall, p. 170

fluency—rapid movement and artistic qualities in the creation of handwritten characters. The lack of tremor or blunt strokes. pp. 25, 26

forensic- the application of science to law. pp. 199, 201

forgery—a non-genuine signature with an intent on the part of its maker to defraud. p. 1
    simple forgery—p. 25
    traced forgery—p. 25
    simulated forgery—p. 25
    cut-and-paste forgery—p. 26

fraudulent—of or pertaining to the deceiving or swindling of someone out of money or possessions; taking without permission, knowledge, or authorization; or distorting or misleading for personal gain. pp. xix, 1, 45, 47, 65

grant deed, p. 131

hacker, p. 169

handwriting habits—those writing features that are unique to each individual as a result of repetition over time. pp. 20, 25

holographic will—a will written entirely by hand and prepared only by the testator. p. 139

"html"—HyperText Markup Language; may also be expressed as "htm." The type of programming language used to create and organize the text and images on World Wide Web pages. p. 172

infrared—literally, "beyond red;" that portion of the light spectrum that is beyond our eyes' ability to see. The dark reds at the high end of the visible light spectrum, which are still barely visible, are approximately 650 nanometers. The human eye cannot "see" light higher on the spectrum, but specialized equipment and filters can. pp. 7, 8, 10, 17, 109

"inkless" fingerprint, pp. 67, 124

invoice, pp. 1, 47

intaglio printing—also called "engraved" printing. It characterizes itself by the ink's being raised above the paper, creating a printed image in relief, such as can be observed on authentic U.S. currency. pp. 74, 84

interlineations—text handwritten in between lines of typewritten text. p. 11

ISP—Internet Service Provider. The company that provides your dial-up account for access to the Internet. p. 179

known writing/document—a signature or writing that was actually produced by a certain person. It is established as a known writing either by admission of the writer, by a witness, or by other means. pp. 14, 20, 138

laid paper—Paper that exhibits faint vertical lines on one side and horizontal texture on the other side. pp. 16, 163

latent writings—invisible impressions on a sheet of paper that are the result of handwriting on a previous sheet of paper that had rested on top of the sheet containing the latent writings. pp. 19, 110, 190

liquidate—to turn negotiable instruments or bank accounts into cash. pp. 2, 45

lithography—see "offset lithography." pp. 5, 61, 74

loupe—a small magnifying device used to determine which printing process was used to create the writings and graphics on a sheet of paper. pp. 74, 82, 87

maker's signature—the authorizing signature of the account holder on the lower right corner on the face (front) of a check. p. 63

mechanical impression—text on a document as a result of a typewriter, impact device, or computer printer. pp. 16, 111, 191

microprinting—the printing of words on U.S. currency and negotiable instruments; these words are so small that they usually cannot be readily seen unless viewed through a magnifying glass. p. 82

mirror-image backup, pp. 165, 167

negotiable instrument—any paper item that can be exchanged for money, whether it be a personal check, cashier's check, money order, warrant, or any similar item that transfers monetary value. pp. 61, 70, 74, 76

notary—a person who is commissioned by the Secretary of State's office to serve as a witness to the signing of documents. The notary may either witness the signing of the document, in which case the notary fills out a "Jurat"—or he or she may only fill out a "General Acknowledgement" affadavit, which is when a person just tells the notary that he or she has previously signed the document but does not sign in the notary's presence. p. 41

notarize—to witness and record the signing of documents. pp. 41, 44

offset lithography—a traditional print-shop method in which a rubber-covered offset cylinder rolls over an inked plate, picking up the ink and depositing it onto the paper. pp. 5, 61, 74

offset printing—see offset lithography.

opine—to give an opinion, ie. when an expert witness gives an opinion in a report or in a courtroom setting.

opponent—the person(s) on the opposite side of a dispute. pp. 11, 37, 198

Paymaster—see "check writer." pp. 5, 69

personalized information—that portion of a check that shows the account holder's name and address. pp. 62, 63

photomicrograph—photograph taken through the eye of a microscope, which process is known as "photomicrography." pp. 9, 33, 39

PIN—"Personal Identification Number"; used to access your bank account at ATM machines. pp. 93, 97, 148

Ponzi scheme—an illegal investment scheme in which a scam artist provides interest or dividends to old investors by using money from new investors. pp. 122, 155

promissory note, pp. 37, 131, 132, 155

proponent—the person who brings forth and offers a document, whether valid or fraudulent, as evidence in a proceeding. pp. 10, 11, 34

questioned document—a document that has come under some dispute concerning the authenticity of signatures, handwritings, mechanical impressions, or other aspects of the document. pp. 13, 14, 192, 198

raised instrument, pp. 52, 85

reconveyance, p. 131

sabotage—the destruction of property to obstruct normal operations; or, treacherous action to defeat or hinder an endeavor. p. 188

security thread—a small polyester thread imbedded into the paper fibers of negotiable instruments and U.S. currency. pp. 72, 76, 82, 84

"short seller"—With reference to the buying and selling of stocks on the stock market, a person who sells a stock short, which is in essence, structuring the purchase arrangement of the stock such that the buyer anticipates that the stock is going to lose value instead of gain value. To "sell a stock short" is to sell it before you buy it. p. 117

SOP—"Standard Operating Procedure;" usually written guidelines used by companies to approach situations consistently and in order. p. 186

skimmer—a small hand-held device that can read and store information from the magnetic stripe on the back of credit cards and debit cards. pp. 90, 147

standards—same as known documents. They are the control samples used in a comparison to questioned writings. p. 11

starter checks—temporary checks issued to a new bank account holder to be used until the printed, "personalized" checks arrive in the mail. p. 177

stylized signature, p. 27

substitution, pp. 10, 33, 36

thermal printing—a printing process in which heat reacts to specially-coated paper to create the printed text. pp. 16, 52, 111

trash marks—see "extraneous toner marks." pp. 15, 36, 184

watermark—impression pressed into paper by "dandy-rolls" during the manufacturing process, resulting in an image that becomes visible when the document is held up to the light. pp. 16, 72, 76, 82, 83

xerographic—from "xero" meaning dry and "graphic" meaning writing; or, "dry writing." The technology used by photocopier machines and computer laser printers, whereby dry toner is fused onto the paper by heat. pp. 5, 163

FURTHER READINGS

Albrecht, W. Steve et al. *Fraud: Bringing Light to the Dark Side of Business.* New York: McGraw-Hill Companies, 1994.

Allen, George B. *The Fraud Identification Handbook.* Highlands Ranch, CO: Preventive Press, 1999.

Bologna, Jack. *Avoiding Cyber Fraud in Small Businesses: What Auditors and Owners Need to Know.* New York: John Wiley & Sons, 2000.

Engel, Peter H. *Scam: Shams, Stings, and Shady Business Practices and How You Can Avoid Them.* New York: St. Martin's Press, Inc., 1996.

Gonzalez, Orlando. *Corporate Fraud Prevention : A Guide to Help Business Owners Avoid Losses.* South Florida Financial Crime, 1998.

Horan, Donald J. *The Retailer's Guide to Loss Prevention and Security.* Boca Raton, FL: CRC Press, Inc., 1996.

Kimiecik, Rudolph C. *Loss Prevention Guide for Retail Businesses.* New York: John Wiley & Sons, Inc., 1995.

Newman, John Q. *Identity Theft: The Cybercrime of the Millennium.* Port Townsend, WA: Loompanics Unlimited, 1999.

Propper, Eugene M. *Corporate Fraud Investigations and Compliance Programs.* Dobbs Ferry, NY: Oceana Publications, Inc., 2000.

Tilley, Bob, et al. *Positive Loss Prevention.* Bob Tilley and Associates, 1999.

Weiner, Alfred N. *How to Reduce Business Losses from Employee Theft and Customer Fraud.* Vestal, NY: Almar, 1998.

If you are interested in further readings specifically in the field of Questioned Documents, I recommend the following books:

Conway, James V. P. *Evidential Documents.* Charles C. Thomas Publisher, Bannerstone House, 1978.

Ellen, David. *Examination of Documents, Methods and Techniques,* 2nd Ed. Bristol, PA: Taylor & Francis, 1997.

HANDWRITING IDENTIFICATION: FORMULA FOR AUTHENTICITY

(Technical Paper presented to the American Academy of Forensic Sciences)

James A. Blanco, Diplomate: A.B.F.D.E.
Blanco Questioned Documents
1006 4th Street, Suite 703
Sacramento, CA 95814

Presented at the 51st Annual Meeting of the
AMERICAN ACADEMY OF FORENSIC SCIENCES
Orlando, Florida
February 19th, 1999

Introduction

This paper will organize and discuss the various areas of handwriting examination into three main categories of Line Quality, Letter Forms, and Letter Proportions. Such examination considerations as rhythm, movement, tremor, construction, angularity, letter forms, character relationships, diacritics, etc. will be arranged under these three headings. Although it is understood that these specifics could be organized otherwise, this arrangement is used to discuss the formula for determining authenticity. While these independent criteria are considered by Forensic Document Examiners in everyday examinations, their relationship in concert is not always clarified in determining when a signature is authentic or forged.

A further matter of discussion will be the importance of the presence of habitual similarities in all three of these areas in order to determine that a signature (or handwriting) is authentic. Conversely, dissimilarities in any one of these areas should get the attention of the examiner, and, in the absence of a reasonable explanation for the presence of such dissimilarities, such handwritings should not be identified. "Simple," "simulated" and "traced" forgeries will also be addressed in relationship to this "formula."

Of course, the purpose of the examination of two or more handwritten items is to determine whether or not they were written by the same person, and, assuming the Questioned Document Examiner has the proper equipment, training and useable evidence at his disposal, and, assuming the comparisons are of questioned writings to known writings[1] , we can proceed with our discussion.

Features Of Handwriting Examinations

When each of us was taught how to write in grade school, the teacher trained us to reproduce the letters of the alphabet as they appeared on the classroom wall and in our writing work books. But after our rudimentary training in handwriting, we were then allowed freedom to "personalize" our own hand and thus began our departures from copybook forms taught in school. As we continued through school, we further incorporated additional distinctive handwriting characteristics into our writing repertoire. These distinctive features manifest themselves in our "adult hand" in different ways. They may appear as the unique manner in which we construct our letters, unique forms, distinctive connections between letters and so on. The following discussion of Line Quality, Letter Forms and Letter Proportions incorporates many of these distinctive writing features under these three main headings.

Line Quality

Line quality considers motion and skill, that is, writing speed, which is also reflected in varying levels of pen pressure. In the consideration of skilled writings, the archaic term "vigor" speaks to the life injected into writings which have been executed rapidly. Such vibrant writings often exhibit artistic quality as observed by their flourishes and embellishments.

Stereo microscopic examination of the writing line using a fiber optic light source from an oblique angle would reveal tapered beginning, internal, and terminal strokes, as well as deep pen track depressions carved into the paper fibers at various points along the pen line. David Ellen writes,

> "When writing is made naturally the pressure applied to the paper is not consistent. Some lines are made quickly and the pen hardly touches the surface, while others, where more change of direction is required, are made with more weight. When the pen is lifted to begin the next word the pressure is progressively reduced and the end of the line tails off gradually. In trying to produce a careful and slowly made freehand copy such variations in pressure are difficult to reproduce."[2]

Conversely, labored forgeries are characterized by even writing pressure throughout, sometimes accompanied by excessive ink deposits. Line tremor, hesitations, pen lifts, blunt strokes, and overwritings are all marks of poor writing skill, if not forgery. Tremor may be defined as,

> "A symptom of forgery manifested as tense, shaky, irregular strokes caused by unnaturally slow pen movements due to conscious attention to letter forms in deliberate rather than spontaneous writing; may also occur naturally in authentic writing due to old age, illness, low writing skill or a variety of external conditions."[3]

An obvious question, then, in the consideration of line quality would be, "Is the tremor due to poor writing ability, disguise, recent trauma to the writing hand, or forgery?" These are the difficult issues that usually clarify themselves given sufficient known evidence and experience on the part of the Forensic Document Examiner. Of course, on the basis of line quality alone, some inferior writers can be excluded as the possible authors of writings which are better than what they are able to produce.

Letter (Character) Forms

The category of letter forms considers the manner in which the character was made and its resulting appearance. This begins with a consideration of "construction," that is, what direction or path did the pen take to "get there" or to "make that"? David Ellen discussed three different ways by which the letter a can be constructed.[4] Although particular letter forms may appear similar, the writing instrument may have taken a different direction in constructing the form.

The resulting product of construction and pen direction is a "pictorial image" that is a certain shape, height, width, and a particular size. The terms "angularity" and "roundness" also apply in as much as these are descriptions of forms.

The fluent "design" of an authentically executed signature is known only to the unconscious hand of the true signer who, indeed, does not even know himself how he signs his own name or what ingredients comprise his authentic signature. All he knows is that the document is placed before him, and in a rapid, thoughtless, yet habitual burst of action, he generates yet another authentic rendition of his own true signature.

The difficulty for the forger in forging a signature is not only to reproduce a gross pictorial likeness of the individual characters themselves, but also, to reproduce the other more obscure details, such as letter construction, and to do so with such a measure of speed as to make the signature line appear fluent. Such a task is too daunting for the forger, as few have both the awareness of the job that needs to be done, along with the skill to do it.

Although a general appearance may be approximated by a forger, the forger would not have been aware of all of the subtleties of pen direction, shapes, and sizes, not to mention the elements of line quality which have already been addressed.

The Questioned Document Examiner needs to exercise particular caution in these considerations when examining stylized signatures. The stereo microscope should be applied to all stylized signatures so that the examiner can decipher details of pen direction in the construction of the forms. Some forgers do a good job in reproducing the form of the letters, but the pen may have taken a different path to create those forms. Such departures from habituality in construction should provide a clue to the Document Examiner that something is wrong with the questioned signature or writing before him.

Letter (Character) Proportions

Letter proportions refer to character relationships to one another. Some characters will appear very close to one another as other combinations of characters will be spaced unusually far from one another. Certain characters may be unusually small or large following other characters.

Height relationships of characters, one to the other, will also vary. Connecting strokes may appear between certain combinations of letters while disconnections will characterize other pairs. The distinctive use of diacritical markings may also provide significant fodder during the examination process.

As to the overall placement of a signature or a handwriting on the document, "base line adherence" is an observation of the writer's propensity to place the writings either above, on, or just under the writing line. Slant is a further consideration of the overall signature or writing.

When examining extended writings, the formatting, spacing, indenting, use of margins, punctuation, habitual spelling errors, use of abbreviations, mixed usage of upper and lower case and/or mixed usage of hand printing with handwriting may all be explored in order to assess the subject's use of written communication. All of these distinctive handwriting characteristics are the result of the writer's habit.

And, of course, since it is commonly understood that even the same writer does not write, for example, his signature exactly the same way twice, the expression "writing variation" also applies to all of the minutia heretofore discussed. That is, in addition to the single occurrences of distinctive handwriting features that we observe in a person's writing sample, there is the further cataloging of any variant forms of the same characters or writing features.

Applying the formula to different brands of forgery.

The forger is not able to reproduce into all three areas the habitual features of the known writer.

It is important to rehearse that the difficulty for the forger in forging a signature or imitating a writing is not only to reproduce a gross pictorial likeness of the individual characters themselves, but also to reproduce the other less obvious habitual details of the writing, and to do so with such a measure of speed as to make the signature line appear fluent. Again, David Ellen states,

> "The problem of achieving a good copy of a well formed and flowing signature is that two conditions have to be met. Firstly accuracy in shape and proportion within the signature is required, and, secondly, smoothness of line. Either one is not too difficult to manage, but, for most people, to satisfy both is nearly impossible."[5]

Simple forgeries (the most common type in law enforcement[6]), are those wherein the forger writes the name of someone else, with no attempt to replicate the pictorial likeness of that person's true and natural signature. For example, if John Smith writes (in his own hand) the name of "Sam Jones," with no effort to duplicate the likeness of a true signature by Sam Jones, then this is a simple forgery. The resulting signature would exhibit rapid pen movement and fluidity evidenced by changes in pen pressure along with tapering. Thus, the line quality of this signature would be considered good. However, the letter forms would not match and the proportions would be dissimilar. Therefore, two elements of the three part formula would be missing. In these cases it is usually obvious to the trained as well as the untrained eye that the "Sam Jones" signature was not an authentic signature by the true Sam Jones. It stands to reason, then, that simple forgeries provide the best opportunity in identifying the forger.

Simulated forgeries are those where the forger copies the likeness of a model signature. The model may be from memory, or the model may be positioned right next to the document being forged. In these situations the forger attempts to duplicate the gross features, that is, the pictorial likeness, of the model signature. Effort is concentrated on letter form (but not construction or pen direction) including height, angularity and perhaps slant. The forger may also reproduce some details of character relationships, connections, and perhaps even base line adherence if the forger is very intuitive. These features are all reproduced in varying levels of accuracy. However, in most simulated forgeries where the forger does a good job of reproducing details of letter forms and letter proportions, he fails to accurately reproduce line quality. The dynamics are that by writing slowly to accurately reproduce the pictorial likeness of the signature, the forger fails to realize that this slow pen movement results in even pen pressure, blunt beginning and ending strokes, lack of striation, and even tremor.

Exceptions to the application of this formula would be where the true writer naturally writes with even pressure and tremor either due to age, illiteracy, damage to the writing hand or medication. Course-of-business handwriting specimens from the victim should bear this out.

In simulated forgeries, different portions of the signature may transition between simple forgeries and simulated forgeries. That is, the forger may accurately reproduce the beginning characters of the given name and of the surname, but would lapse into their natural hand throughout the remaining characters of the given and surname. In these cases, the application of the formula for authenticity would apply at different junctures of the questioned signature. Referring back to our example of John Smith writing the name "Sam Jones," the "S" in Sam and the "J" in Jones would be pictorially accurate with a reduction in line quality. The "am" and "ones" might be rapidly executed and therefore exhibit good line quality, yet the details of accurate letter forms and letter proportions would be missing.

Traced forgeries are those where a model signature is placed on a light table (light shines through the source document from behind) and the document to be forged is placed on top. The forger then follows the line of the model projected from behind as he traces the forgery on the document above. Although these signatures may appear very accurate in their reproduction of letter forms and letter proportions, they lack tapering in their beginning and ending strokes and appear as a drawing since they were slowly executed using even pen pressure. Some tremor in the writing line as well as uniformity in the width of the pen line both testify to this signatures lack of vitality. What this signature gains in pictorial similarity of the letter forms and letter proportions, it loses by virtue of its dissimilarity with the line quality of the authentic signatures.

Conclusion

Of course, there are exceptions to all rules. However, these are general guidelines in the approach to determining the authenticity of signatures. When questioned signatures or handwritings are authentic, they should exhibit the same level of writing ability as determined from examinations of line quality of the known specimens. Further, authentic writings should exhibit similarity in letter forms to include the same features of construction. And finally, commensurate letter proportions between questioned and known writings will testify to authenticity. In the comparison of questioned writings with known specimens, when sufficient distinctive handwriting similarities exist in all three categories of line quality, letter forms and letter proportions, then, barring the presence of unexplainable differences, we can know that such questioned writings are indeed authentic.

1. See 1.1 under Purpose, TWGDOC/SWGDOC SOP's, *Guidelines For the Examination of Handwritten Items* Number 10 (Rev. 12/98)

2. *The Scientific Examination of Documents*, David Ellen, Second Edition, Taylor & Francis 1997. p. 35

3. From "A Glossary Of Terms For Document Examiners" compiled by Carl McClary (ATF Lab Atlanta)

4. Ellen, Ibid; p.16

5. Ellen, Ibid; p. 35

6. *Evidential Documents*, James V.P. Conway, 1959, Charles C. Thomas, Third printing, 1978, p.28

DOCUMENTS AFFECTED
BY FORGERY

The California Penal Codes section on forgery (470 (d)), appearing below, describes the different types of documents affected by forgery.

"...any check, bond, bank bill, or note, cashier's check, traveler's check, money order, post note, draft, any controller's warrant for the payment of money at the treasury, county order or warrant, or request for the payment of money, receipt for money or goods, bill of exchange, promissory note, order, or any assignment of any bond, writing obligatory, or other contract for money or other property, contract, due bill for payment of money or property, receipt for money or property, passage ticket, lottery ticket ...trading stamp, power of attorney, certificate of ownership or other document evidencing ownership of a vehicle or undocumented vessel, or any certificate of any share, right, or interest in the stock of any corporation or association, or the delivery of goods or chattels of any kind, or for the delivery of any instrument of writing, or acquittance, release or discharge of any debt, account, suit, action, demand, or any other thing, real or personal, or any transfer or assurance of money, certificate of shares of stock, goods, chattels, or other property whatever, or any letter of attorney, or other power to receive money, or receive or transfer certificates of shares of stock or annuities, or to let, lease, dispose of, alien, or convey any goods, chattels, lands, or tenements or other estate, real or personal."

DESCRIPTION OF THE TERM "FORGERY"

California Penal Code's description of Forgery (470. Acts constituting forgery) is very lengthy, but I have placed some highlights here in Appendix D.

"(a) Every person who, with the intent to defraud, knowing that he or she has no authority to do so, signs the name of another person or of a fictitious person to any of the items listed in subdivision (d) is guilty of forgery."

Further,

"(b) Every person who, with the intent to defraud, counterfeits or forges the seal or handwriting of another is guilty of forgery."

And,

"(c) Every person who, with the intent to defraud, alters, corrupts, or falsifies any record of any will, codicil, conveyance, or other instrument...is guilty of forgery."

The laws regarding forgery and fraud are not limited to the Penal Code. In California, these laws extend to the Business and Professions Code, the Corporation Code, the Government Code and the Insurance Code.

As you can see, the word "forgery" has a broad definition and an even more encompassing application. The reason that the code is so descriptive is that so many people have been ripped off that the writers have tried to be clear as to what forgery and fraud can be. In fact, recently-retired Detective Bill Cramer re-defined and updated these codes in the California legislature a few years ago, also clarifying the more modern applications of fraud using computers.

ABOUT THE AUTHOR

James A. Blanco is an independent Examiner of Questioned Documents certified by the American Board of Forensic Document Examiners. His client work ranges from police departments to insurance companies to businesses of many kinds and sizes. His 17-year plus career in the field includes forensics positions with the Sacramento County California Sheriff's Department, the U.S. Treasury Department (Bureau of Alcohol, Tobacco and Firearms) and the California Department of Justice. He flies his own plane to research questioned documents or testify in trial cases all across the United States, and also in Canada and Mexico. He lives in Sacramento, California.

He may be contacted via his website: **www.PreventFraud.net**